BETH MOORE

WALKING *with* GOD

A FIVE-WEEK JOURNEY IN STEP WITH THE SAVIOR

TYNDALE MOMENTUM®

A Tyndale nonfiction imprint

Visit Tyndale online at tyndale.com.

Visit Tyndale Momentum online at tyndalemomentum.com.

Visit the author online at lproof.org.

Tyndale, Tyndale's quill logo, *Tyndale Momentum*, and the Tyndale Momentum logo are registered trademarks of Tyndale House Ministries, registered in the United States of America. Tyndale Momentum is a nonfiction imprint of Tyndale House Publishers, Carol Stream, Illinois.

Walking with God: A Five-Week Journey in Step with the Savior

Cover design by Libby Dykstra

Interior design by Laura Cruise

For information about special discounts for bulk purchases, please contact Tyndale House Publishers at csresponse@tyndale.com, or call 1-855-277-9400.

ISBN 979-8-4005-1017-5

Printed in the United States of America

32 31 30 29 28 27 26
7 6 5 4 3 2 1B

To you, fellow traveler, on this journey of faith—

I wrote my first Bible study over thirty years ago without having any idea God would see to a second one. Twenty-something studies later, the wonder of getting to walk with someone through the pages of Scripture to know and grow in Christ has never waned. I never take this privilege lightly, nor even one of you for granted. You matter to me. I thought of you with every word I wrote. Go forward, loved of the Lord, whether you are new to the study of Scripture or a seasoned student of many years. When your life in this mortal body is nearing its end and the veil of heaven is wearing thin, you will look over your shoulder at the winding path behind you and not regret a single step you took with Jesus.

With great affection,
Beth

....

With overflowing gratitude to the immensely gifted Stephen Proctor, my co-conspirator in countless live events, bringing themes in Scripture to life on screens. What tremendous joy to now partner with you in print. Your photographic artistry and creative eye mark this book with a sacred beauty that invites a willing reader into worship. What could be more meaningful? I dearly love you, Stephen.

Contents

INTRODUCTION

The Walk Ahead

My co-laborers and I at Living Proof Ministries work in a marvelous and inviting three-story home refurbished into an office building. Chalk it up to thin walls, creaky floors, wide air-conditioning vents, a good set of ears, or a combination of the four, but from a certain spot on the top floor where I study and write, I can hear what's happening all over the building.

"Isn't that a tad distracting?" you might ask. Well, yes, sometimes, especially if my coworkers are laughing, because I hate to miss anything funny. *Why don't you sit somewhere else?* you'd understandably wonder. Because I like it. I'm an extroverted writer, which is nearly an oxymoron. I spend copious hours alone. I love hearing them nearby.

Fact is, I not only recognize my coworkers' voices and distinctive laughs, I also know their footfalls. Without hearing a single word from their mouths, I could tell you with a strong measure of accuracy which of my eleven staff members is walking across the fake hardwoods of our second story. I know from the rhythm, the sound of the gait, the pace (usually a matter of short or long legs), and the kind of shoes they're wearing.

That's Kimberly, I'll say to myself with a smile as her heels *click*, *click*, *click*, quick, quick, quick down the hall, her being short-legged and all. Or *That's Dana, and I think she's walking into Sabrina's office*. Dana's also on the shorter side but walks with a very deliberate stride. She doesn't go anywhere she doesn't mean to go. *Ah, first-floor Mary's come up to the second floor*, I'll say to myself. *She's usually heading to Sabrina's office, but I think she just stopped off at Jenn's*. Mary almost always wears flats, but she purposely tries to walk without disturbing anyone—which gives her away, of course. I feel the need to say that Jenn's legs are a good five inches longer than anyone else's on the second floor, so I never miss on her.

Surely you get where I'm going with this. We humans walk differently from one another. To be sure, commonalities exist. We have legs and feet or crutches, wheels, canes, or walkers, for instance—not that walking with God requires physical mobility. We can, and often do, "walk" with God from a chair, desk, couch, or bed, and thankfully, some very close walking with God can take place from a hospital bed or a deathbed. All we need is a willing spirit. We will often draw comparisons to the physical act of walking in this study, however, because they can lend insight into the spiritual act. Beyond a few basic commonalities, the way individuals walk can be quite distinctive, and these distinctions are most recognizable to the ones who know us best.

I have a bit of a limp from tearing my right knee teaching aerobics a thousand years ago. Keith was kind enough to point out its persistence to me after watching me teach not long ago. "I forget how you limp until I'm sitting in an audience watching you onstage." This explains why I rarely take him to my speaking engagements. A dear friend of mine walks unevenly too, but not over an injury. One leg simply outgrew the other. Another friend is the peaceful sort who is never in a hurry. She walks with all the haste of a tablespoon of molasses rolling toward a biscuit. This explains why I try to meet her wherever we're going, lest I forget why I like her before we arrive.

We're converging in these pages for one supreme reason: We want to walk with God. And if we've already been walking with God, we're likely here because we don't want to quit, don't want to lose interest, and very much do want to walk nearer and more attentively with our Maker. You're also in the right place if you at least wish you wanted to walk with God. If the phrase "walking with God" is even on your radar, welcome! It's on mine too.

What to Expect over the Next Few Weeks

We won't make it past the book of Genesis before we begin to suspect what bears true throughout the biblical canon: No two people described in Scripture as walking with God appear to have done so identically. We'll also find, sometimes to our great frustration, that a walk with God doesn't always look the same from season to season even in an individual's life. Further, walking with God will not always seem like a forward march or an advancement in our faith. A stretch of miles when God seems gloriously obvious can be followed by months of wondering where he's gone. God has his own objectives for each season of our walks, and some of them will remain a mystery until we see his face.

For this reason, different days in the pages that follow may look different over the course of these five weeks. Some require more writing from you, some less. Some include a challenge to take a certain action. In the fourth and fifth weeks, for example, you'll be asked to interview a person whose walk with God you admire, much like the interviews I've included as part of this study.

God willing, some of these activities will spark an awareness of God's interest and nearness in pleasures that are simpler but deeper than the ones this insatiable, ensnaring world sets before us. Wouldn't it be wonderful, for instance, to hear ourselves think again? And, even better, to hear the thoughts of God again through his living words? What if we could recapture some sanity and stability over these five weeks of walking with God?

This entire study is inviting us into a deeper embrace of what Brother Lawrence, the seventeenth-century Carmelite friar, meant by "the practice of the presence of God"—a way of being he developed in a monastery kitchen.[1]

The accompanying video sessions and workbook chapters will take us into five eras of the biblical storyline to help us catch glimpses of what a walk with God looks like.

- Our first week will have us primarily in Genesis.
- Our second week will direct us to the other Books of the Law.
- Our third will plant us in the Psalms and a few other selections of biblical poetry.
- Our fourth, the Gospels.
- Our fifth, the Epistles.

An Invitation to Keep Company with Jesus

A couple of years ago in preparation for a Bible lesson, I happened on some phraseology put to paper by Eugene Peterson that would not let me go. It's a description the pastor-scholar included in his commentary on the books of 1 and 2 Samuel to capture the approach of early Christian writers and teachers to Old Testament readings. You'll find it at the end of this excerpt.

> From the very beginning of the church's life, Christians have read the Hebrew scriptures in a way that understood that God's revelation in Jesus was implicit from the outset. Our earliest Christian writers and teachers were fond of using the phrase "before [or "from" or "since"] the foundation of the world" to insist that what God revealed of God's self in Jesus was not an afterthought, something tacked on, but was in place and operative from the beginning. . . . And so our Christian ancestors read these Samuel narratives while keeping conscious company with Jesus."[2]

While keeping conscious company with Jesus. These words arrested me upon the first reading and have etched themselves into the way I now think. Imagine this becoming the way we read Scripture: *keeping conscious company with Jesus*. Imagine this becoming how we perform our jobs, our duties at home, and our menial tasks: *keeping conscious company with Jesus*. Imagine this becoming the current for how we conduct our relationships and overlook offenses and love our neighbors and enemies alike: *keeping conscious company with Jesus*. Imagine this becoming the way we gaze at a country landscape, a piece of art, a flowering tree, an ocean tide, or a cooing infant: *keeping conscious company with Jesus*. What if we started seeing the marginalized, oppressed, harassed, and poor while *keeping conscious company with Jesus*?

What Brother Lawrence meant by practicing the presence of God is, in my estimation, similar in concept to Peterson's idea of keeping conscious company with Jesus. Both communicate the concept of living intentionally—to the degree a human is able—in God's good company. Our aim is similar throughout these five weeks. We're not seeking to master a spiritual discipline. If such were attainable, the purpose would be defeated. We're not trying to get good at something over these five weeks.

We're after what John called fellowship with the Father and the Son through the Holy Spirit (1 John 1:3). We're after the practice of divine communion that is to be savored when discernible and to be counted on when not. Here we are pursuing a life confident that God's promises are true even when we, like our forefathers and foremothers of faith described in Hebrews 11, will see some of them only on the distant horizon.

If you've done one of my earlier Bible studies, expect parts of this one to read a little less like my standard curriculum. In previous studies, I wished I had the space here and there to depart from the format and elaborate from a personal standpoint like I would in a regular book. Because our walk with God is the hub of every spoke in the life of faith and because I believe nothing on earth to be more stabilizing, I took the liberty this time, writing with a more blended approach. You'll still read and respond to Scripture in every lesson. You'll also find commentary excerpts and meanings of Hebrew and Greek words where they add richness to our understanding. But I've placed deliberate emphasis on spiritual formation and mentoring (meaning not just "what" but "how") and, for the reader who could use some nurturing in Christ, a sliver of spiritual mothering.

How to Use This Study

So, as you turn these pages, think *Bible study meets book*. Use the chapters ahead, the corresponding video sessions, and the bonus interviews any way you find helpful.*

*  *Bonus interviews available to watch here.*

If the intensity is part of what you like about a study like this one, seek to finish it in five weeks. If you'd rather slow down and take extra time to absorb the material, by all means, set your own pace! It's yours to use any way you see fit, but try to keep up the momentum. That's without a doubt the way to get the most out of it.

At the beginning of each week, you'll find a listening guide with blanks that corresponds with a video lesson I've taught to launch the week. If you're not able to view or listen to the message, skip the listening guide and proceed to day 1.

God's "silence" never means absence.

Every exercise included in this study—in the Scripture passages, in the questions to answer, in the spaces provided for journaling, and then on the pavement putting it into practice—is meant to enrich our walk with God. If we are in Christ, we are in a relationship with a God who can be known intellectually and spiritually, who can be sought and studied, but also a God who can, on his own terms in his own time, be *experienced*.

At his own sovereign will and pleasure, God makes his nearness more obvious at times. He might cause us to perceive a divine enablement of some kind. He may fill us with an otherworldly joy or cause tears of gratitude to stream down our faces over something we can't even articulate. He may delight us with the beauty of a phrase in Scripture or give us a sudden knowledge of what direction we should take. He may flood our anxious soul with an alien peace. He may send someone our way to confirm to us how much we are loved and seen by him.

God is no less present, his promises no less true, when he is utterly imperceptible. On the same note, God's "silence" never means absence. I'll reiterate these truths to you as we go. The fact is, I believe God is willing to reveal himself more often than we, in this overstimulated culture, have the attention span to notice. One of our objectives is to become more attentive and God-aware so that, if and when Jesus has a mind to make us particularly aware of his activity or his answers to prayer, we won't miss him.

I'm so glad you've picked up this book. Writing it has been deeply meaningful to me. I suspect God held this theme back from me until I'd hobbled near him long enough to hold little back from you. I have much more to learn in my walk with him, but whatever I have to give is yours, whether I learned it from praying and studying Scripture in times of delight, desperation, or daily grind; whether I learned it from walking through failures or successes with God; or whether I learned it from the observations of others or personal experience. At my age, you come to appreciate them all as graces, and as always, God's graces are abundant enough to both keep in full measure and share generously.

I believe to the marrow of my bones that the good life is the God-life. Those who make it their chief aim to walk with God through their brief earthly tenure will end up—sometimes accidentally—fulfilling divine purpose, doing good works, and receiving consolation in their suffering, *even if they don't recognize them as such until they see the face of Christ*. That which is to the glory of God is, by his sovereign plan and endless mercy, also for the good of people. The deep conviction I write from is that what is best for us—Christ Jesus over all, in all, and through all—is also the most satisfying and joy-giving life, and one well worth living.

Let's go ahead and muster up the faith that what we hope for—a closer, more discerning, more perceptible, more obedient, and fruitful walk with God—is on the divine agenda for us.

In Christ Jesus,

Beth

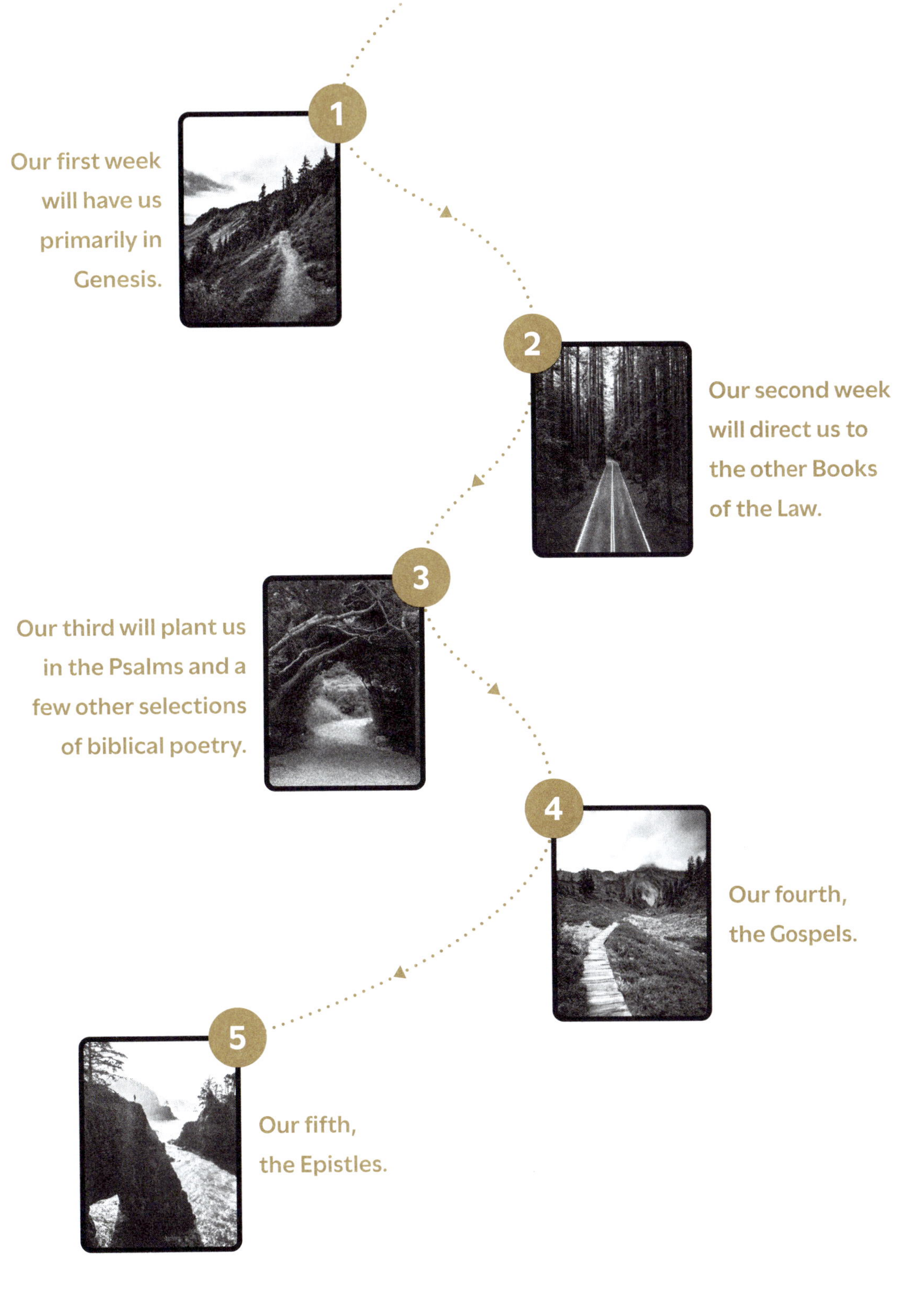
1
Our first week
will have us
primarily in
Genesis.
2
Our second week
will direct us to
the other Books
of the Law.
3
Our third will plant us
in the Psalms and a
few other selections
of biblical poetry.
4
Our fourth,
the Gospels.
5
Our fifth,
the Epistles.

WEEK 1

the BEGINNING *of* WALKING

SESSION 1

The Beginning of Walking

You can fill in these blanks as you watch the video for session 1.

__________________: In each of our five weeks together, our goal will be to gain insight into what walking with God looked like in a particular era of biblical history in order to enrich our understanding and appreciation of walking with God in our own.

1. The ____________ of walking is ______________________________. Glance at the first several chapters of Scripture as they move toward Genesis 3:8. Walking with God _________ as the _____________ of __________________ God.

   Read Genesis 5:1-24.

2. The mention of ________________________________ means to stop careful readers in their tracks. (Compare Hebrews 11:5-6.)

   See Genesis 13:14-18 and Genesis 17:1 for the third figure we find walking.

3. Note the CSB translation *live* rather than *walk*. The two words are also used somewhat interchangeably in translations of the New Testament. They aren't, however, entirely synonymous. ____________ lends itself more readily to the notion of _______________.

הָלַךְ (*hā·lăḵ*): v. (qal) go, travel, i.e., ________________________ to another place, with any form of transportation (2 Ki 7:14); (piel) travel (Ps 104:26) . . . (hitp) go about (Zec 1:10) . . . (qal) walk, i.e., make linear motion on foot or pod (Lev 11:20); (piel) go about (1 Ki 21:27); (hif) cause to walk (Lev 26:13); (hitp) walk about, . . . (qal) follow, i.e., make linear motion behind another object or collection (Ge 32:20); . . . behave, conduct, ________, formally, walk, i.e., go about doing certain actions in a regular, more or less consistent manner, so possibly _________________________ or lifestyle, as an extension of the act of walking as regular and patterned (Lev 20:23).[1]

4. One paradox of the gospel's ________________ is found in its _________________________.

No story is told as big and bold as the one God tells in Scripture. To human eyes, the plot may hide, but it is never lost. Just when you think it so, keep reading and watch it rise from the ashes. It could blow in with the next wind, get picked up by a caravan, float on an ax-head, ride in on a camel, hurl from a slingshot, or burst from a grave. What the story will not do—cannot do—is die. Leave the tome on a shelf to collect an inch of dust, and the pages inside will still teem with the story of life everlasting.

Open the cover of your Bible without turning to any particular page. Simply let it lie open for a moment, and give thought to the wonder there at arm's length. That's no ordinary book, you know. And you do. That's why you're here. And why I'm here. But how unordinary is it? Whether you're just beginning to crack the spine of a Bible or you've spent years inside the pages, no time is the wrong time to ruminate on its uniqueness. How we read what we read frequently determines where it leads. We'll devote this opening lesson, therefore, to exploring that deep, existential question shrugging the shoulders of preoccupied humans:

Why bother?

Specific to the task at hand, why bother with Bible study? I'm serious. Who among us needs one more time-consuming thing to do? Not one of us. Who among us needs divine help to juggle responsibilities, navigate relationships, sort out problems, deal with health issues, love prickly people, resist bitterness, forgive wrongs, be forgiven for wrongs, get back up, start all over, and tumble once again into transcendent joy that somehow makes all the trouble of living worth it? I do. You too?

NOTES

DAY 1

Your instructions are a doorway through which light shines.

PSALM 119:130, NET

You know you're alive. You take huge steps, trying to feel the planet's roundness arc between your feet.

ANNIE DILLARD, *PILGRIM AT TINKER CREEK*

There's nothing better than an open heart before God with an open Bible in our hands. Scripture shows us what a walk with God looks like and plants the road signs that direct our course. So let's stir up some fresh appreciation.

Let's start with the remarkable patience of God eternal in the gradual transmission of the Scriptures. Psalm 90:2 reads,

Before the mountains were born,
before you gave birth to the earth and the world,
from eternity to eternity, you are God.

God has always been, is presently being, and ever more shall be. Long before God, in the poetic language of Moses, "gave birth to the earth and the world," he knew to the minutest detail how he would reveal himself and his redemptive plan to humanity. All things are at his command, so he can use whatever he pleases, but in the Bible's unfolding, we find God revealing himself and communicating his presence and desires to humanity through a variety of means. He uses divine speech ("and God said . . ."), creation and the created order, prophetic speech ("the word of the Lord came to . . ."), natural and supernatural events, signs, wonders,

There's nothing better than an open heart before God with an open Bible in our hands.

miracles, dreams, visions, divine and angelic visitations, sounds (thunder, trumpets, etc.), unusual sights, fire, clouds, a donkey, rain, absence of rain, silence, messages through prophets, and, most importantly to us, written words inspired by the Holy Spirit (Scripture) and the coming of Jesus, the Son.

Since Christ—the Word (Greek *logos*), or full expression, personified logic, exact representation, and perfect revelation of God, himself fully God—is eternal in both being and knowing, the words of God can be understood as eternal. In the diction of Psalm 119:89, "LORD, your word is forever; it is firmly fixed in heaven." Isaiah 40:8 reads, "The grass withers, the flowers fade, but the word of our God remains forever." Christ himself said in Matthew 24:35 (NIV), "Heaven and earth will pass away, but my words will never pass away."

The eternal words of the Eternal Word.

We don't deify the Bible, of course. A pious form of idolatry is still every atom idolatry. Christ, *the Word*, is God, but the Scriptures are not. Their inestimable worth, authority, and reliability are in their divine inspiration and intention. Reflect on the thought that God would communicate to his image-bearing creatures through the sacred pages before ever fashioning a human body and breathing life into it. He knew the artful means of how—a stylus in mortal fingers moved by the Holy Spirit—and the schedule of when. God felt no urgency to blurt all he had to say in one breath. The one who is timeless owns time and, therefore, took his sweet time inspiring the Scriptures. Divine revelation is many things, but God in a rush isn't one of them.

Up for a little history? The Protestant Bible, comprised of the Old Testament and the New, is a progressively revealed library of sixty-six books written over some 1,500 years through the inspired pens of more than forty human authors, then ultimately bound into one volume with one overarching message: a self-disclosing holy God seeking and saving fallen humans at the highest personal cost.

Even after the final word of Scripture was inscribed on a scroll (possibly but not definitely the book of Revelation), God apparently wasn't stressed by a publication deadline. The canon as we know it, with thirty-nine Old Testament books and twenty-seven New Testament books, was not fully recognized by the church as such until around AD 400, after substantial deliberations and debates over authenticity and standards for acceptance.

In the centuries following, copies of the Scriptures were carefully guarded rarities, handwritten by scribes in Latin and placed primarily in the hands of educated clergy and elites. Translations into other languages like English awaited the invention of reusable type-printing in the fifteenth century and the courage of individuals so determined for the Bible to be in the hands of common people and congregations, they were willing to die for it. William Tyndale, the linguist, scholar, and relentless reformer first to translate the Hebrew and Greek biblical texts into English, was strangled and burned at the stake as a heretic in 1536 around age forty-two. As is often the case, his driving passion was born from the birth pangs of great frustration. His issue with the religious machinations of his day is evident in the following words attributed to him:

> In the universities they have ordained that no man shall look on the Scripture until he be nozzled in heathen learning eight or nine years, and armed with false principles with which he is clean shut out of the understanding of the Scripture.[2]

Perhaps the most quoted statement of William Tyndale is one he aimed like an arrow straight toward the tip of the ecclesiastical ladder: "If God spare my life, ere many years I will cause a boy who drives a plough to know more of the scriptures than you do."[3]

Ultimately, God did call Tyndale to give his life for the cause, but not until the type was set for plough boys—and girls—to hold the Book in their callous hands and read it. The Bible is a marvel, you see, and from this perspective, with a side helping of imagination, you might conclude the cover you just opened is no run-of-the-mill book cover. Picture a door swinging open—not to a fairy tale nor a Narnian land beyond a wardrobe, nor a shadowland of ghostlike spirits, but to the world of the Scriptures, infinitely larger and more fascinating than the earth spinning beneath our feet of clay and the atmosphere over our heads.

God begins the story with the creation of the material world. **Turn now to the opening chapter of Genesis and read verses 1-31. Record the material elements created on each "day." Feel free to generalize on the lengthier sections.**

DAY ONE

DAY TWO

DAY THREE

DAY FOUR

DAY FIVE

DAY SIX

Beginnings are meant to be remembered, rehearsed, told and retold. God seemed intent from the start to introduce himself as the one who created all things out of no things in order that, among other things, the clay on its most coherent day might see the absurdity of telling the Potter how to spin his own wheel. Turn to chapters 38 and 39 of the book of Job for a clear example. Job is believed by numerous biblical scholars to be one of the oldest books in the Bible, if not the very oldest. If they are accurate, think how apropos a beginning: God, in effect, saying, "Let there be light" on the existential crisis of suffering.

Note the format of the words in Job and how it differs from the predominant paragraph structure of Genesis 1. Though whispers of poetry are there all along in Genesis 1 and some scholars believe that it, too, was intended to be read lyrically, here in this section of Job we behold the Lord blatantly as poet. **Slide your index finger slowly down the lines of Job 38 and 39, and pick several portions you find arresting. Then read them aloud. (Try to always read poetry aloud.) Which ones did you choose?**

"All Scripture is inspired by God and is profitable for teaching, for rebuking, for correcting, for training in righteousness" (2 Timothy 3:16), but some portions of the Bible are sheer art, meant to hold the gazer's gaze, not just sharpen the student's mind. Job appears among the former, no less than a masterpiece. In these chapters, we feel the emotion, see the fireworks, hear the morning stars singing, and sense our heads swimming to the whirling of planets. The chart of Genesis 1 gives way to the art of Job 38–39. Job's verses aren't looking to be diagrammed, charted, and parsed so much as they are begging to be heard. Wrestled with. Rehearsed. Imagined. Experienced. Wept over. Dreaded. Rejoiced over. Treasured. Tossed and regathered.

Lord, how am I to read this?

Which expression of the Creator's work is better, Genesis 1 or Job 38–39? Both are essential. Both are God-breathed. In this case, the prose and the poetry are both beautiful, but they approach the reader from different angles and carry varied rhythms. Commands don't read like proverbs. Narratives don't read like epistles. Again, how we read what we read frequently determines where it leads. Sometimes the best question is "Holy Spirit, how am I to read this?"

Walking with God is attempting, however awkwardly and certainly imperfectly, to keep in step to some degree with God's rhythm and reason on any given day and in any season. One way we may do this is in Bible reading. You may set out to read two or three chapters and find yourself instead absorbed by a single passage or fixated on a phrase. Other times, you may plan to take it nice and slow and instead get swept up in a fast-moving narrative and keep reading for the next half hour. In either case, was the goal unmet? The answer depends on whether the goal was checking the box on an exact length of Scripture reading or engaging with God in the reading. Yielding to the Spirit's pace isn't always obvious, but it is the most satisfying.

Our walks with God don't happen on a preprogrammed treadmill. They happen in the real living, where next week's calendar is maddeningly theoretical. This tandem walk is comprised of communion meant to move at God's discretion, which the human is tasked to discern by faith and not by sight. And thus, the ebb and flow. Keep in mind the words of Paul in 2 Corinthians 3:17:

> Now the Lord is the Spirit, and where the Spirit
> of the Lord is, there is freedom.

Walking with God assumes certain practices like prayer and Bible reading, but if we slip into automatic, where the method and pace become strictly routine, we can walk on for miles and months without any real involvement with God. In these pages, engagement exceeds regimen. Perhaps the simple phrase "walked with God" in Genesis, used in reference to Enoch and Noah, holds two keys that help unlock the pace.

See it for now not only as a phrase but as three separate words that comprise the phrase. **Record something each word indicates to you.**

WALKED

WITH

GOD

Walking speaks to consistency. (Pick up the feet, put them down. Do it again.) *With* reminds us that we're not alone in this—that Immanuel is with us. *God* in the opening of Genesis is the title associated most with the majestic Creator. Then, might we be helped by thinking along these lines?

Walking with God blends consistency and creativity.
It is a consistent walk with an immeasurably creative God.

In closing, turn your attention back to the first chapter of Genesis. This time, we'll read Robert Alter's translation of the first four verses:

> When God began to create heaven and earth, and the earth then was welter and waste and darkness over the deep and God's breath hovering over the waters, God said, "Let there be light." And there was light. And God saw the light, that it was good, and God divided the light from the darkness.[4]

Welter and waste and darkness. God breathes over the deep, then order—creative, kaleidoscopic, and spectacular—starts taking form out of chaos. I love to imagine that his breath still hovers over the words he breathed on the sacred page in the expanse of time. I like to ask him to make the words warm with his breath as I read and to bring them to life inside my bones and marrow. My way of talking to God may not and need not be yours, but do dare to ask him in your own words to work supernaturally in your life through the Scriptures. Do ask God to open your eyes so you can see the wonders in his teachings (Psalm 119:18) and open your mind to understand the Scriptures (Luke 24:45). The God with whom you're invited to walk is no small God. Nothing is too difficult for him.

Whatever you do, keep the words of God near the heart of God, where they belong. We can read the print and miss the point. Jesus confronted a group of deeply devoted students of the Holy Scriptures in John 5:39-40, 42 with these unsettling words: "You pore over the Scriptures because you think you have eternal life in them, and yet they testify about me. But you are not willing to come to me . . . I know you—that you have no love for God within you." Let that sink in not as condemnation but as caution not to miss the heart of God in the words of God.

The books bound together within this sacred library we call the Bible far exceed a collection of ancient scrolls for display in glass cabinets of museums. Pull a Bible from a box in the attic of a ramshackle house, and it may appear a relic of a bygone era, with long-gone relevance and the vitality of a corpse. Should the discoverer blow the dust off the flaking bonded leather, open its thin pages with frayed edges to the middle, and dare to read a psalm or two, however, she might well find wording for something that needed saying that very morning. The Scriptures are living, breathing words, given by the Holy Spirit and kept alive and vivified by the self-same Spirit in the hearts of humans with a fleck of faith.

The door to the world of the Bible is wide open to you. Come on in.

DAY 2

The LORD God planted a garden in Eden, in the east,
and there he placed the man he had formed.

GENESIS 2:8

Dear Lord, grant me the grace of wonder. Surprise me, amaze me, awe me in every crevice of your universe. Each day enrapture me with your marvelous things without number. . . . I do not ask to see the reason for it all: I ask only to share the wonder of it all.

ABRAHAM JOSHUA HESCHEL

What if, over the coming weeks in this study, we read our Bibles with an even higher objective than learning scriptural principles and developing godlier behaviors? To be sure, both ends are important. A disciple is a learner. We can't grow if we don't learn, and we can't walk with God with a hint of consistency if we don't learn how he walks. As for godliness, only a person out of touch with the God of the Bible can kid herself into thinking how she lives makes no difference to God. But my hope is for someone to discover that both objectives—growing in the knowledge of Scripture and in godliness—more often than not end up naturally accompanying an authentic and deliberate walk with God.

You are my hope, Lord GOD,
my confidence from my youth.
I have leaned on you from birth;
you took me from my mother's womb.
My praise is always about you.

PSALM 71:5-6

One of our high hopes here is to learn to lean and, in doing so, realize that in leaning we learn. Think of the young shepherd David penning the words to his God: "thy rod and thy staff they comfort me" in the twenty-third psalm (KJV). The shepherd's staff had multiple features, but certainly among them was a sturdy bend and break-resistant cane, or shillelagh, on which the weary, the overworked, and the weak could lean. Think also of the beloved disciple, who leaned against Jesus at the supper table that last evening before Jesus' crucifixion (John 13:21-28). What if we also saw our Scripture reading and Bible studying as dining with Christ on the feast of his words and, rather than only sitting classroom style (a good thing), we often sat supper-style and scooted in (an even better thing)?

The benefits of reading Scripture are boundless. No need to choose a few. The supreme purpose of the sacred words, however, is to reveal to us the saving Word who is Christ the Lord. Above all else, the highest, most crucial aim of every spiritual discipline—indeed, every life practice in a journey of faith—is to know Christ, to be drawn by the Spirit into deeper, more satisfying, sanctifying communion with him, to be fed and led by him. In a nutshell: to walk with God. This is something Cece Winans has experienced, as you'll see in our interview this week.*

I'm proposing that, throughout these five weeks, every time we open our Bibles, we pause and ask the Holy Spirit to quicken those words and bring them to life in a way that is enlightening and transforming—perhaps at times even transfixing and mesmerizing—to us. Let's ask the Holy Spirit to teach us, inform us, convict us, show us, direct us, thrill us. When it comes to the work of the Holy Spirit, the words of James 4:2 could hardly be more applicable:

You do not have because you do not ask.

To make the connection, read Luke 11:9-13. What is Jesus encouraging his followers to do?

....

....

....

Fill in the remainder of Luke 11:13. "If you then, who are evil, know how to give good gifts to your children, how much more will the heavenly Father ____________________

____?"

*  *Find Beth's interview with Cece Winans here.*

Ask for all of it these next five weeks. Ask for every good thing the Lord is willing to show you and work in you. I'm talking about the things of real value. Of eternal value. Not the eroding things of this world. Ask him for the filling and satisfaction of his Spirit. For the riches of understanding and insight. For wisdom and creativity. For love and joy and faith. For more fruitfulness in your calling. Start asking him to fill the empty places in you with himself, to the full measure. Ask him to cause the seeds of the Word he'll implant in your soul to have a profound yield, "a hundred times what was sown" (Luke 8:8). Why not ask?

Isaiah 7 records a most intriguing dialogue between the Lord and King Ahaz. The Lord says to Ahaz:

"Ask for a sign from the LORD your God—it can be
as deep as Sheol or as high as heaven."

ISAIAH 7:11

Can you imagine God encouraging you to ask for a sign from him and making it virtually limitless? How would you respond? Well, this is the way Ahaz responded:

"I will not ask. I will not test the LORD."

ISAIAH 7:12

"But, Ahaz," we'd protest, "the Lord just told you to!" According to the prophet Isaiah, the refusal of Ahaz greatly tried the patience of the Lord. He'd send a sign anyway, but with no pleasure in the king. In Luke 11, Jesus does not tell us to seek signs, but he does indeed exhort us fervently to ask of, seek from, and knock on the door of our gracious heavenly Father for the good and lasting things of the Holy Spirit and of the Kingdom of God. **So, with an asking, seeking, and knocking frame of mind, turn to the third chapter of Genesis and read verses 1-13. After you've completed your reading, meditate on verse 8.**

The man and his wife heard the sound of the LORD God
walking in the garden at the time of the evening breeze.

God walking. Since we've been invited into this anthropomorphism, let's go with it. Here we're invited to imagine a God who has legs, and two legs as opposed to four, mind you. God did not create the beasts of the field, the fish of the sea, or the birds of the air in his image. God is wooing us in this scene to picture him with feet. The Lord alone knows to what extent we can stretch the anthropomorphism without it snapping, but questions blow the dust off stale imaginations, even if they have no answers.

Here are a few. In the time prior to the fall in the garden, can we confidently assume that the man and his wife had seen their Creator's actual form? Did God in the nascent era take on the likeness of humanity with a body that could be touched? Did his feet leave prints in the dirt? We don't actually know, but don't you wish we did? Sometimes the attribute most asleep in our Bible study is curiosity, and if we're to appreciate what is meant by walking with God, it needs waking up.

What we do know is that God walked among them in the garden in a way that could be *heard*. "The man and his wife heard the sound . . ." This singular detail suggests a tangibly impactful form that, if applied to anything else, assumes some measure of weight. If you walk through a stretch of woods often enough, you'll likely learn to distinguish the sound of a rabbit or a raccoon, a deer, a dog, or a person, only the last of which, if you're like me, raises any real caution.

Sometimes the attribute most asleep in our Bible study is curiosity.

The point to be drawn is that hooves sound different from paws, and both sound different from feet. Large sounds different from small. The whistling of a human is distinct from the whistling of the wind through the trees. In the narrative of Genesis 3, the man and woman crouching in an effort to be unseen recognized God's approach purely from sound.

The messianic passages of Isaiah 53 lead us to picture Jesus as rather unremarkable in size and appearance. How God chose to reveal his presence "in the beginning" is less clear. To be sure, Adam and Eve recognized the Lord God moving among them was not their peer . . . except, perhaps, for one enticing moment when the serpent suggested he was. That fateful day, the couple didn't hide from a being they could take on. They knew more vividly than ever that the one they were dealing with was wholly other.

The Hebrew word for "glory" in the Old Testament is *kavod*. The term conveys weightiness. Think in terms of market trade in antiquity and how the value of a particular item—be it fruit, grain, liquid, stone, or precious metal—was ordinarily estimated by weight. When we use the idiom "worth their weight in gold," we're calculating according to this ancient measure. We don't know precisely how God revealed himself to the man and woman in the garden, but this much we can count on from the expanse of divine revelation: God's glory is immeasurable. His full weightiness cannot be weighed.

The man and woman bought what the deceiving serpent was selling at an incalculable cost. These were people who, before that fateful day, got to live out of their truest identity and fullest security and highest satisfaction. They fellowshipped with their Maker and with each other in a paradise designed for exactly such a purpose.

Let me ask you this: Have you ever gazed at a magnificent piece of art while standing

next to the artist? If so, when and what was the experience like? If not, what do you imagine that experience would be like?

I've had the privilege of standing inches away from contemporary artist and Jesus-follower Makoto Fujimura and looking at one of his paintings with him.* I'd seen it just minutes before he walked in the room. Next to him, however, the interpretation became clearer, and the colors and textures took on entirely new extravagance. I've heard poems read so powerfully and poignantly by the poets who wrote them that I wept. I've heard excerpts from books read aloud by their authors in such a way as to change the way I read their work from then on. The ones who write the words know every intended pause and the precise pace. They know the interpretation. They know the schematics. How much more, then, does God know his own work? Imagine beholding the masterpieces of the universe while standing in the presence and company of the Master. Come near with the faith of a child.

Master, why did you choose to make the horse neigh, the cow moo, and the donkey bray?

What were you thinking when you made a porpoise twirl and a whale frolic and a seal clap?

Master, why did you design a mango to taste this way and a papaya to taste that way?

What did you do out of necessity for creation, and what did you do for the pure fun of it?

I hope one day to ask God some of these questions and endless others. Consider also how he will answer what we didn't know to ask and show us what we didn't know could be seen. Imagine gazing at a mountain in his good company and God saying something like this: "What you see before you isn't all there is. Come with me." Now, imagine he takes you by the hand and leads you into a cave. You bend your body and make your way through a narrow tunnel

* 

Find Beth's interview with Makoto Fujimura here.

and into an open space where you can stand upright, and suddenly the light of your escort's presence dances on the surfaces of a thousand icicle-like stalactites.

Just think of the conversations we have coming when we're finally in God's perceptible presence. Now, imagine being Adam and Eve and, instead of having such unspeakable privileges of presence *coming*, you're seeing it *going*. The loss would be a living death.

What specific reason is given in Isaiah 45:18-19 for God's creation of planet Earth?

Consider the particularity of our planet in comparison to others in our solar system. **What are a few of the conditions that make the earth more inhabitable than say, for instance, Venus or Mars?**

Might it be fair to say that God formed the earth to be inhabitable most exquisitely by humans in order to enjoy them, bless them, and fellowship with them? Would we be going too far to suggest that God designed humans intellectually, emotionally, spiritually, and physically distinct from all other creatures so he could walk with them rather than simply watch them walk? By his sovereign wisdom, God also fashioned mortals with freedom of choice, refusing to force them to enjoy his presence or plug their ears to seductive voices threatening to lead them astray. This is no God of oppression. The arms of this God stretch wide open with invitation.

DAY 3

Though the mountains move and the hills shake, my love will not be removed from you and my covenant of peace will not be shaken.

ISAIAH 54:10

Fear is just courage's preamble. When we practice remembering that the Spirit of Christ is our companion, fear simply becomes one more prompt to pay attention to the voice . . . of Love. Fear doesn't have to be an enemy to conquer. It can be a place to be companioned by Love.

K. J. RAMSEY

I've been on the same journey as countless others among us in recent years, disoriented over the burgeoning hate, wrath, extremism, racism, depravity, irrationality, brutalization, and polarization overtaking what seems every conceivable realm in our society. **Did I overlook a social ill you've found particularly bewildering? If so, add to the list:**

Ours is a social, political, and religious world we humans have managed to fashion in our own image and, I believe, inadvertently under the influence and authority of "the ruler of the power of the air, the spirit now working in the disobedient" (Ephesians 2:2). Faced with such an escalation, we naturally become solution oriented.

- What do we need to do to fix this?
- In this ever-widening fracture, how can we find our way back together?
- What should be the first response of the church?

So we start trying to come up with ideas.

- We need revival!
- No, we need an awakening!
- No, we need better discipleship!
- No, we need to preach the gospel more clearly!
- No, we need a sermon series on unity!
- We need to disfellowship!
- No, we need to re-fellowship!

And on and on we go, trying to solve the problems as if we truly know what is causing them. We are right to pray for, plead for, seek after, and work toward resolutions to solvable problems, but we're mistaken to think we can stop this fallen world from falling. The burgeoning problems we see haven't materialized ex nihilo. They are the outgrowth of deeply entrenched troubles ignored—whether accidentally, conveniently, or out of a feeling of helplessness—until they've gained momentum that's hard to miss.

How do we navigate a virtually unrecognizable world? How do we find a path through a dense forest of poisonous trees with branches enough to eclipse the sun? And how do we keep from eating their low-hanging fruit when our taste buds are acclimated to it? First, we must recognize that not all poisonous fruit tastes like poison. A time comes when we're forced to face how we like the way some poison tastes. We realize we're not just the affected. We're the infected. With this realization comes good news. When we begin to face the true condition of our culture, our own disordered affections, worldly absorptions, and personal contributions to the madness, and resolve to look to God and the Scriptures for a better way to live, we're already pivoting northward.

Today we'll peruse the life of an individual who was surrounded by a world woefully harder to navigate than ours. First, the context. **Read Genesis 6:5-7. Flip back to Genesis 1:26-31 and review the wording. Note the stark contrast between the two segments. In what ways do you see a reversal of sorts in Genesis 6:5-7?**

According to Genesis 6:5, "human wickedness was widespread on the earth" and "every inclination of the human mind was nothing but evil all the time." Endeavor to grasp such an invasive darkness engulfing us today. We wouldn't have the luxury of combing through movie or series titles to find remotely decent entertainment, because such a thing would be impossible to find. Imagine the cruelty and public depravity of a society populated by people at their worst. Covering our children's eyes from sights they lacked the maturity to process would be impossible. Anyway, unless we were Noahs among our godless contemporaries, our own inclinations would be so evil we wouldn't care what kind of exposure our children had. Imagine never being astonished to learn what has been happening behind closed doors because there are no closed doors.

Take a quick look at Galatians 1:4. How does the apostle Paul refer to the era in which they lived (and we also live)?

In the same letter, however, Paul spoke eloquently about concurrent realities in this present age, like the transforming power of the gospel, fellowship with other believers, the fruit of the Holy Spirit in frail human beings, and the ability to bear one another's burdens. Though this is a "present evil age," we can't accurately claim that every human inclination and motivation is only evil. Yes, we see cruelty, injustice, rampant deception, and depravity, but in the lamplight of God, we can also behold goodness and beauty in this present darkness.

As a reminder that the world hasn't entirely been swallowed up by a dark, gaping abyss, offer two or three examples of oppositional good often on display in your personal sphere of living. I'll mention a few to get you started:

- Our children's choir at church and the way they search the sanctuary for a parent or grandparent the moment they're on stage and how they wave
- The toothy smile and unbridled enthusiasm of a teenage sacker at our grocery store who has Down syndrome
- A friend who hosts baby showers for single moms in crisis

Your turn:

To deepen our appreciation of the details when Scripture offers them and to widen our landscape for walking with God, let's take a moment to backtrack. In our opening session, we dropped into the fifth chapter of Genesis to catch a glimpse of the life of Enoch, a man who presents a remarkable case study in walking with God. Enoch and Noah appear in subsequent chapters in Genesis and in subsequent verses in Hebrews. Let's follow suit and view them, one after the other. Take Enoch first. **Read or review both Scripture segments—one from the Old Testament and the other from the New—and extrapolate every detail you can find about Enoch. Record them under the coinciding references.**

ENOCH	
Genesis 5:18-24	Hebrews 11:5-6

Draw lines between any details offered in the Old and New Testaments that either blatantly or subtly lend insight to the other. Now take the same initiative regarding Noah in the next chapter of Genesis and the next verse of Hebrews. Read both portions, then comprise your lists and draw lines between links.

NOAH

Genesis 6:5-14

Hebrews 11:7

The case studies in the Bible of mortals walking with God come in a refreshing array of conditions and characters. Keep this in mind when you're tempted to think your walk with God should perfectly replicate your mentor's or peer's. He didn't weave our DNA, design our frames, mold our minds, shade our skin, and distinguish us from all others by the print of our thumbs because he is most glorified by duplicates.

In an early summer Sunday-morning sermon at the Metropolitan Tabernacle in Newington, Charles Spurgeon's voice shook the room in his iconic Spurgeon style. His text? Genesis 5 and 6, and a segment of Hebrews 11. His emphasis? The distinctions between two men who walked with God: Enoch and Noah.

> We may take pleasure in thinking of Noah as a kind of contrast to Enoch. Enoch was taken away from the evil to come, he did not see the flood, nor hear the wailing of those who were swept away by the water-floods. His was a delightful deliverance from the harvest of wrath which followed the universal godlessness of the race. It was not his to fight the battle of righteousness to the bitter end, but by a secret rapture he avoided death, and escaped those evil days in which his grandson's lot was cast.
>
> Noah is the picture of one who is the Lord's witness during evil days, and lives through them faithfully, enduring unto the end. It was his to be delivered from death by death. The ark was, so to speak, a coffin to him, he entered it, and became a dead man to the old world, and within its enclosure he was floated into a new world, to become the founder and father of a new race. As in the figure of baptism we see life

by burial, so was it with this chosen patriarch, he passed by burial in the ark into a new life.

In Enoch we see a type of those of God's people who will go home peacefully before the last closing struggle. Ere the first clash of swords at Armageddon, such Enochs will be taken from the evil to come. But in Noah we see those who will engage in the conflict, and bear themselves bravely amid backsliding and apostasy, until they shall see the powers of evil trodden under their feet as straw is trodden for the dunghill.[5]

What part of Spurgeon's excerpt is a new thought for you?

A few common denominators in the lives of the two individuals would almost certainly exist, whether they are specified in Scripture or assumed. **What do you think a few of those would be?**

Capture a description of Noah offered in Genesis 6:9 (CSB) by filling in the blanks:

These are the family records of Noah. Noah was a righteous man, ...

....;

Noah walked with God.

Noah wasn't superhuman, and to be certain, he wasn't sinless. Scripture teaches that no one is without sin but the triune God. Noah was, however, a righteous person and "blameless among his contemporaries." The adjective *righteous* means much of what you'd expect:

> It is nearly always used of persons, either men or God, and often stands in contrast to "wicked," רשע. Near synonyms include "innocent" and "upright." In legal contexts, "righteous" means "innocent" or "acquitted" of specific offenses, e.g., Exod 23:7-8; Deut 25:1. More generally, a righteous person is one who keeps the moral law: Ezekiel defines the righteous man as one "who does what is lawful and right" and then goes on to give examples of sins he avoids and good acts he does, e.g., clothing the naked and feeding the hungry, 18:5-9.[6]

The Hebrew word translated "blameless" in Genesis 6:9 includes a meaning we're less likely to associate with our English word. As Dr. Gordon J. Wenham explains,

> "Blameless," תמים, is a term much more rarely applied to people than "righteous." The root idea is that of wholeness or completeness.[7]

Noah was wholly God's. Given over completely to him. He wasn't perfect, but he withheld nothing of his imperfect human self from his God. His reputation belonged to the Lord. No small thing. People would have thought he'd lost his mind. His labor belonged to the Lord. His family belonged to the Lord. His community belonged to the Lord. His future belonged to the Lord. His well-being and the well-being of everyone and everything he loved—you guessed it—belonged to the Lord. What a beautiful concept of blamelessness: being unable to find a cell in that body or a whit of his soul without "the Lord's" firmly engraved on it. We're not hard pressed to imagine what an impact this kind of holistic surrender would have on a human's walk with God. **Reason briefly in this space how blamelessness would be rarer than righteousness.**

As we draw today's thoughts to a conclusion, let's meditate on the phrase from Genesis 6:9, "among his contemporaries." The prophet Isaiah offers important insight into the Lord's attentive order in this verse. Read the words carefully.

Who has done this and carried it through,
calling forth the generations from the beginning?
I, the LORD—with the first of them
and with the last—I am he.
ISAIAH 41:4, NIV

The Lord has called forth every generation from the very beginning, and he knows exactly which generation will be present on this earth when Christ returns and his Kingdom comes for every eye to see. Psalm 33:11 assures us, "The counsel of the LORD stands forever, the plans of his heart from generation to generation." Psalm 145:13 tells us God's "rule is for all generations. The LORD is faithful in all his words and gracious in all his actions."

Not one generation will slip past God's notice. This point carries significant weight in our walk with God because we will be tempted at times—as will the next generation, the next, and the next—to think faithfulness is utterly impossible in a world this corrupt. We'll tend to imagine God lowering the bar in light of our present darkness. Keep ever before you and train up the next generation to be assured that the time will never come when God will be overwhelmed by evil, detached from his throne, no longer watching, no longer faithful, and no longer well able to make his people well able to serve him. Let our contemporaries be what they may. As for us, let us give ourselves wholly to the Lord, withholding nothing, and let us walk with God, wobbly though we may, until he walks us home.

DAY 4

You yourself have recorded my wanderings. Put my tears in your bottle. Are they not in your book?

PSALM 56:8

Can I invite Jesus in to all of that? And if I do, what will happen?

MALCOLM GUITE, *THE WORD IN THE WILDERNESS*

Today is set aside to introduce and acclimate you to a record-keeping method for weekly practice that God will make increasingly meaningful to you as you get into the rhythm of it. Nothing about the exercise is arbitrary or a waste of labor. Think of the page as a sketch pad for developing the art of God-awareness. As you become more aware of God, you'll see how intimately he is aware of you. He longs to awaken you to more of what he's doing in and around you, enlarging in you what the apostle Paul prayed for us all: "That the God of our Lord Jesus Christ, the glorious Father, would give you the Spirit of wisdom and revelation in the knowledge of him . . . that the eyes of your heart may be enlightened so that you may know what is the hope of his calling" (Ephesians 1:17-18).

You will almost certainly see that he is with you more than you've known, actively engaging with you, desiring you to become more aware of his ways and means as he teaches and reveals himself to you, conveying his love for you. If you actively engage in the practice, your eyes will open wide to what he's showing you in small things we're prone to miss in all our preoccupations. These revelations don't clear up the mysteries, but they become the kinds of things that carry us when we have no explanation for the mayhem happening around us. All we know is that Jesus is right here with us, and that singular truth is the literal difference between day and night.

Written remembrances have been incorporated into lives of faith for centuries and, in fact, from the very beginning. Ours is a record-keeping God. Your Bible is evidence that God does not simply speak. He *records*. He did not leave us to oral tradition alone in matters of highest priority. God equipped us with words on pages. Genesis 2:4 illustrates the connection beautifully: "These are the records of the heavens and the earth, concerning their creation. At the time that the LORD God made the earth and the heavens . . ."

Under the direction of divine inspiration, the book of Genesis also offers a record of family lines with a place of significance in the story of faith. **Circle every appearance of the word *records* and underline who the records pertain to. Draw a star by the name *Abraham* where it appears.**

- "This is the document containing the family records of Adam. On the day that God created man, he made him in the likeness of God" (Genesis 5:1).
- "These are the family records of Noah. Noah was a righteous man, blameless among his contemporaries; Noah walked with God" (Genesis 6:9).
- "These are the family records of Noah's sons, Shem, Ham, and Japheth" (Genesis 10:1).
- "These are the clans of Noah's sons, according to their family records, in their nations. The nations on earth spread out from these after the flood" (Genesis 10:32).
- "These are the family records of Shem. Shem lived 100 years and fathered Arpachshad two years after the flood" (Genesis 11:10).
- "These are the family records of Terah. Terah fathered Abram, Nahor, and Haran, and Haran fathered Lot" (Genesis 11:27).
- "These are the family records of Abraham's son Ishmael, whom Hagar the Egyptian, Sarah's slave, bore to Abraham" (Genesis 25:12).
- "These are the names of Ishmael's sons; their names according to the family records are Nebaioth, Ishmael's firstborn, then Kedar, Adbeel, Mibsam" (Genesis 25:13).
- "These are the family records of Isaac son of Abraham. Abraham fathered Isaac" (Genesis 25:19).
- "These are the family records of Esau (that is, Edom)" (Genesis 36:1).
- "These are the family records of Esau, father of the Edomites in the mountains of Seir" (Genesis 36:9).
- "These are the family records of Jacob. At seventeen years of age, Joseph tended sheep with his brothers" (Genesis 37:2).

References to Abraham and his family line are always significant because God chose him as the first of the Hebrew patriarchs. We'll touch on this a bit more in our next lesson. **What is an additional reason Abraham's line should have significance to us, according to Galatians 3:29?**

Scripture itself is evidence of the value God places on recording elements, experiences, and events relevant to faith in him. Mind you, because of his great mercy ultimately displayed on the cross of Christ, God keeps no record of wrongs, for . . .

> If you, LORD, kept a record of sins,
> Lord, who could stand?
> But with you there is forgiveness,
> so that we can, with reverence, serve you.
>
> PSALM 130:3-4, NIV

One of the most mesmerizing sections of Scripture conveying God's penchant for record-keeping is found in Malachi 3:13-16. **What had some of the people spoken against the Lord?**

Do their complaints have any relevance in our current culture? If your answer is yes, how so?

We know the Lord knows all things, but what we're meant to not miss in this segment of Scripture is that he overhears people talking about him. There's simply no talking behind an omniscient God's back. On the flip side, we see in the same section this marvelous reference to a heavenly amanuensis sitting before the Lord keeping records in a volume called "a book of remembrance." **What is being recorded?**

Let that sink in for a moment. Every time we boast in the Lord and speak to another person or to other people about his love, goodness, grace, kindness, and power, God inclines his ear, listens, and has it recorded in a book. The thought of such divine attentiveness is astonishing.

Needless to say, a universe of difference stretches between God's infinite, inspired, and accurate recordkeeping and ours. The suggestion is that written remembrances are part of our faith tradition and still of great value. Now, let's get to the tutorial. Once you get the hang of the exercise, I think you'll savor it.

Turn to the chart at the end of week 1. You'll find seven labeled spaces. This chart appears at the end of each of our five weeks. What and how much you'll record in the boxes each week will naturally differ. Let's familiarize ourselves with the categories to heighten our awareness concerning what kinds of things we want to write down. Any time throughout the course of each week that you have something to record under one of the categories, do so while it is fresh on your mind. Leave room for other entries in the remaining part of the week.

You need not fill in every category every week. This is not a test where you make a lesser grade if you leave a blank. The aim is to keep a record of moments that capture your attention so you can reflect with God on them at the close of each week.

Staying in the present is one of the most important parts of the exercise. A mindset attentive to the "now" tends to be the weakest for most of us. We are often, understandably, more preoccupied with the past and the future than the present. Incalculable value comes from looking back at our history with God and seeing how faithful he has been to us. We will certainly have occasion to do that in these five weeks. Equally, trusting God with the concerns about the future is crucial to our faith walk. We will likewise have occasions to do that. But this weekly recordkeeping is intended to help us become more oriented to our present, daily, and weekly walk with God. This is the muscle that often needs strengthening most.

Remember in the introduction, where I wrote about Brother Lawrence practicing God's presence and Eugene Peterson commending the early Christians for keeping conscious company with Christ even in texts of the Bible where he is not specifically mentioned or inferred? I likened the goal of this study to both. But here a disclaimer of sorts is due: We will never, in this lifetime, perfect practicing God's presence or constantly keep conscious company with Christ. Brother Lawrence and Eugene Peterson knew it too. These records, however, give us a chance at the end of each week to reflect on keeping conscious company with Christ, if not in real time, *shortly after*.

Get what I'm saying? We'll reflect with the Lord, thanking him for the blessings, delights, and insights we experienced or encountered and setting before him our sighs and laments, knowing he cares and hears us, and asking him to tend to us. We'll thank him in advance for his faithfulness, sufficient grace, and divine power in the areas of our sorrows and sighs.

The idea is to record each entry as soon as possible after experiencing, noticing, or encountering it so you don't forget. You will continue to make entries throughout the week, then be encouraged to reflect on them at the end of each week. At the conclusion of the study, you will look back at all five charts and record any observations, if you're willing or, at the very least, marvel over God's goodness. I believe you'll find the exercise to be deeply meaningful—for reasons neither you nor I know to anticipate.

Here are the categories and explanations where greater clarity might be needed.

Delights

List things that bring you particular delight as they happen. Anything at all that simply brings happiness and gladness or laughter to you. As you reflect on these week to week, they will produce the marvelous fruit of gratitude.

Here are a few examples to get you started:

- The taste of something delectable
- The discovery of a bird nest with eggs
- A newborn fawn
- Running into an old friend
- A baby's smile
- A breathtaking sunset
- A full-circle moment
- Something or someone making you laugh until your sides hurt

Few things are more delightful to me than sitting under the stars around a fire on a cold night roasting marshmallows with my family. I'm persuaded that all good things are from the Lord, so have no fear of crediting him with more than he actually did.

> Every good and perfect gift is from above, coming down from the
> Father of lights, who does not change like shifting shadows.
>
> JAMES 1:17

Perplexities

This category could seem awkward at first, but it may turn out to be the one you end up enjoying most. This space is for recording things you find puzzling. Keep in mind, perplexity is not always negative. You may be perplexed by a sight or a conversation, for example, or a Scripture verse or a current event that simply makes you wonder. On the other hand, someone may react strangely to something you said, leaving you perplexed. Whether in negative or positive contexts, you can spot a perplexity by the quick leap to the questions "What was that?" and "What does that mean?" A key reason why we record the most notable of these week to week is that God sometimes brings surprising clarity.

Remember, curiosity is an asset in a walk with God.

> They were all astounded and perplexed, saying
> to one another, "What does this mean?"
>
> ACTS 2:12

Sighings

A few things you might note under this category:

- A longing (yet again?) unfulfilled
- A hope deferred
- A closed door
- A missed opportunity
- An unresponsive friend
- Intimacy rejected

Lord, my every desire is in front of you;
my sighing is not hidden from you.
PSALM 38:9

Laments

Lament can overlap significantly with sighing, but for our purposes, we'll distinguish between them on our chart using two factors. (1) **Intensity.** For example, think of the difference between what makes you sigh and what makes you sob. Think of sighing primarily in terms of a response to disappointment and bewilderment. On the other hand, consider lament a response to more severe theological disorientation, to disruption of life with the potential to disrupt faith. (2) **Direction.** Lament is voiced (inaudibly or audibly) *to*, *toward*, or *about God*, whereas the sighings we bring to God could be about anything. Lament is an earnest complaint to the Lord himself and is made sacred by its honesty and intimacy. Nothing about a lament is faithless. You can hardly complain to a God you don't believe exists or possesses the power to act.

I cry aloud to the LORD;
I plead aloud to the LORD for mercy.
I pour out my complaint before him;
I reveal my trouble to him.
Although my spirit is weak within me,
you know my way.
PSALM 142:1-3

Divine Consolations/Comforts

This section is for recording moments week to week when you're inclined to think God has tended to you in a way deliberately meant to comfort or console you. A particular verse of Scripture in your reading that day might seem a particular comfort from God in your circumstance, hurt, loss, or disappointment. An unexpected gift, a call, a word of courage, a sublimely beautiful day, a meal dropped off at your house, a spontaneous and warm embrace—all qualify as divine comforts when we yearn for reminders of God's nearness and awareness of our need. The arrival of a friend can be one such comfort. The apostle Paul spoke of such a consolation:

God, who comforts the downcast, comforted us by the arrival of Titus.
2 CORINTHIANS 7:6

Several friends sent me a butterfly bush after my beloved big brother's sudden death last year, and I planted it by his memorial on our property. It thrived remarkably, shooting from some eighteen inches high to four feet tall and wider still in one year. It blooms prolifically and gives me the strangest comfort in my grief. I've voiced my gratitude and sent pictures to my friends numerous times, but I also thank God who used them to soothe my sorrows.

> When I am filled with cares,
> your comfort brings me joy.
>
> PSALM 94:19

Perceived Presence

This category is for recording times you believe you particularly sensed the presence of God in your midst. You may be understandably reluctant to record anything under this heading in fear of presumptuousness or in case you are mistaken. Most of us have looked back on a time we thought God was manifesting his presence in some remarkable way only to later conclude the experience was more likely spiritual or emotional manipulation, whether deliberate or well meaning. These experiences can lead us to maturity and deeper discernment, but let's not follow them down the rabbit hole to shame, cynicism, or unbelief. God can do anything he wants. He can show up anywhere and in any way he wants. Let's guard against coming to the fraught conclusion that God never makes his presence known in perceptible ways.

The Bible records copious occasions of manifest presence. God knows our interpretations are not always accurate. He doesn't condemn us for wanting to experience him so badly that we read more into a setting than is there. No doubt we err every bit as often by missing his presence and chalking up anything noteworthy to coincidence or human doing. What you record in this box is your perception, not perfection. It's about possibilities, not just certainties. You're a human with finite understanding, longing to meet with God in a way that you can perceive on a sensory level. You're not getting a grade. Our purpose is to walk more alertly and gratefully and attentively with God.

> The one who has my commands and keeps them is the one
> who loves me. And the one who loves me will be loved by
> my Father. I also will love him and reveal myself to him.
>
> JOHN 14:21

Word Alerts

We'll use this category for recording Scriptures that land on us with particular significance to our season or to a matter at hand, whether that seems to be a direction from the Holy Spirit, a confirmation of some kind, a warning, or simply a sense that we're to take note of it and trust God to bring understanding later. Jot down the scriptural reference with a short note beside it to remind you why it seemed significant. This section is set aside entirely for insights from Scripture. Words from other resources and people can be greatly encouraging, but record those in one of the other sections. Here we want to distinguish between the words from within Scripture and words outside Scripture that are often rich and insightful but not God-breathed.

> The revelation of your words brings light
> and gives understanding to the inexperienced.
> PSALM 119:130

As we near the end of our time together in this first week, go ahead and record anything fresh on your mind that fits one of the categories, and do likewise on day 5. In weeks 2–5, you'll have the entire week to make entries. This recordkeeping will have residual blessings, as it will not only help you mark the Lord's intervention now but will also serve as a stone of remembrance in the future.

DAY 5

Your father Abraham rejoiced to see my day;
he saw it and was glad.

JOHN 8:56

This is my Father's world
He shines in all that's fair
In the rustling grass I hear him pass
He speaks to me everywhere.

MALTBIE D. BABCOCK

We'll finish our week on "The Beginning of Walking" and our readings in Genesis with one of the most astounding examples of walking with God in the Old Testament. The scenes involve Abram (later Abraham), the man God called to leave the house of his father, Terah, in the Mesopotamian city of Ur and set out to a land that would be shown to him. "I will make you into a great nation," God promised Abram. "I will bless you, I will make your name great, and you will be a blessing . . . and all the peoples on earth will be blessed through you" (Genesis 12:2-3).

He'd have offspring, God said, in numbers rivaling the stars. The problem was, Abram and Sarai couldn't even come up with one measly child. They took matters into their own hands, as we humans are wont to do, and Abram conceived a child with Sarai's servant, Hagar.

The results were disastrous, of course. The women turned on each other. An innocent child was trapped in the middle of a triangle of adults acting like children. Thirteen years later, Abraham was ninety-nine when the Lord appeared to him and said,

I am God Almighty; walk before me faithfully and be blameless. Then I will make my covenant between me and you and will greatly increase your numbers.

GENESIS 17:1-2, NIV

Circle the phrase "I am God Almighty," and underline "walk before me faithfully and be blameless." We looked briefly at Genesis 17:1 in our opening session. Today we'll follow the narrative a bit further to make a most memorable walk connection.

In Genesis 17, God commands Abraham and his offspring to be circumcised as a sign of the covenant and reassures the old patriarch that the promise remains despite their best human efforts to thwart it. Abraham pleads for Ishmael to be the accepted heir and, though God denies the patriarch's request, he promises to bless Ishmael and make him into a great nation.

The events recorded in Genesis 18—the segment meant to draw our focus today—occur shortly afterward. This chapter in the book of beginnings circles us back to the concept of walking in the second scene, but let's not miss the offerings of the first scene. Read Genesis 18:1-8.

Who "appeared to Abraham at the oaks of Mamre"?

According to 18:2, what did Abraham see when he looked up?

Genesis 18:9-15 records a conversation more delicious than the meal. **First, record a significant shift from a plural reference to the inquirers in 18:9 to a singular reference in 18:10.**

Who in her right mind wouldn't have eavesdropped on this conversation? I'd have tripped all over Abraham's ancient feet bringing in a tray of tea . . . then sugar cubes . . . then scones . . . then, "Silly me, I forgot napkins!" After all that, I'd drag in the vacuum and head straight to the floor beneath the Lord's legs. Anything to hear what he had to say. Or was it "they" who had something to say? We'll get back to that quandary in a moment. Sarah, the paragon of self-control, however, stayed hidden at the entrance to the tent. She'd have gotten away with it, too, had the visitor not said something she found so absurd.

> I will certainly come back to you in about a year's time, and your wife Sarah will have a son!
>
> GENESIS 18:10

That did it. She burst out laughing. The Lord called her on it, then made one of the most glorious, consequential statements in holy writ—one that echoed throughout. **Write the question the Lord asks in Genesis 18:14:**

Is it, my friend? Anything at all? Do you need to be reminded of this in the worst way for any reason? Or, on the other hand, does it almost make you mad because you've been let down before and you don't want to hope, only to be disappointed once more? **Expound on your reaction, if you're willing.**

Now, how about we get to the part where we see the walk connection? **Read Genesis 18:16-22. Succinctly record what happens in this scene.**

God is better than he has to be.

I'm sure you caught the usage of our key word *walk*. Notice that God told Abraham in Genesis 17:1 to walk before him faithfully. In this scene, however, he is not just walking *before* him. He's walking *with* him. God's call to walk before him faithfully finds ample significance in our journey of faith. To walk before God is to journey onward, ever mindful of being in the divine presence, sought out, seen, and fully known by our Maker. But no greater privilege exists on this rocky soil than to walk *with* God.

If you've ever taken a child to a park and watched him play with other children and seen him glance in your direction from time to time to reassure himself of your nearness, you can relate to having a loved one play before you. But you'll agree that the engagement level increases if, instead of having you watching from a nearby bench, the child requests that you push him on the swing. In this case, the child is no longer in your watchful care only but actively moving in response to your push. The child has gone from playing before you to playing with you. The same is true in the act of faith walking.

Now, pick back up at Genesis 18:22. How many of the visitors are left with Abraham at this point?

This scene in Scripture is among those meant for beholding with wonder more than exegeting with dogma. I'll tell you what I wonder, however. Three visitors showing up at Abraham and Sarah's tent amid references to "the LORD" would, at first blush, make me think they could represent the Trinity: the Father, the Son, and the Holy Spirit, three in one. However, in verse 22, two of them leave the scene, and we're told Abraham is left standing before "the LORD." This detail leaves me to wonder, since the one who remains with Abraham is identified as the Lord, if the two others are cherubim disguised as men. See if you think the idea has merit based on the following verses. **Look up each one, then record any pertinent information:**

Isaiah 37:16

Exodus 25:22 (To increase your wonder, see John 20:11-12 in view of Exodus 25:22.)

Hebrews 13:2

Don't you love seeing those kinds of connections? **Our final reading today is Genesis 18:23-33. Briefly describe what is happening in these verses.**

The seemingly inexhaustible capacity for sin possessed by the conscience-seared people in Sodom and Gomorrah was by no means limited to sexual exploits. **In what other ways had they heaped sin upon sin, according to Ezekiel 16:49-50?**

Does God's inclusion of Abraham's inquiry bring you comfort, like it does me? I'm convinced of this to the marrow of my bones: We will not trust who we cannot question. We can admire, esteem, and enjoy individuals we can't question, but we won't fully trust them and we certainly won't want to entrust ourselves to them. We may have a boss at work or a leader we revere in a church or faith community, but if questions are off-limits or concerns are met with offense or withdrawn favor, trust will flee, distrust will seed, and suspicion will grow.

In one of the most fascinating dialogues in the biblical canon, the mortal Abraham's part of the conversation is built entirely on inquiry. **His question in Genesis 18:25 is worthy of recording in this space:**

The answer to the question is *yes*. The Bible conveys God's unwavering wisdom and righteousness from cover to cover. The fact is, however, hundreds of other questions will go unanswered over the course of our mortal lives. But the fact that we have the God-given right to ask will prove essential to our trust. To be allowed to fall to the floor upon learning of a tragedy and cry out with bitter tears, "How could you let that happen?" without fear of being struck dead by our Creator is no small right.

Questions are allowed in a walk with God. Encouraged, for the love of all things holy. Necessary for intimacy. Trying to swallow them down when they need to come up is like gulping unbelief. Your thoughts are read by God like an unrolled scroll, and not one word, doubt, or question makes you a whit less loved. "Perfect love drives out fear" (1 John 4:18).

Delights

Perplexities

Sighings

RECORDKEEPER FOR YOUR WALK

Laments

Word Alerts

Divine Consolations/Comforts

Perceived Presence

WEEK 2

the LAW *of* WALKING

SESSION 2

The Law of Walking

You can fill in these blanks as you watch the video for session 2.

Introduction: In our first session, we focused on the genesis of walking with God: God himself walking in the garden with the man and woman he'd created in his image. We've been challenged to adopt the audacious faith of Enoch, who believed he could walk with God in *some way* if not the *same way* as Adam and Eve before the fall. In this session, we shift to the next era, shedding significant light on the biblical history of walking with God.

Here we'll consider the ________________________.

Read Leviticus 26:1-8 to set the context, then follow it with Leviticus 26:9-13, filling in these blanks according to the CSB translation.

> 9 I will turn to you, make you fruitful and multiply you, and
> confirm my covenant with you. 10 You will eat the old grain of
> the previous year and will clear out the old to make room for
> the new. 11 I will place my ____________ among you, and I
> will not reject you. 12 I will ______________________ and be
> your God, and you will be my people. 13 I am the Lord your
> God, who brought you out of the land of Egypt, so that you
> would no longer be their __________. I broke the bars of your
> yoke and enabled you to _________________________.

1. God walking among a people is a close-up, ___________________________________ to individuals to walk with him.

2. In matters of faith, _______________ is not _____________. Compare Revelation 2:1.

3. A ___________ of walking with God always leads to an _____________.

4. The divine ___________________ we call ____________ is how ________________ learn to ______________________.

Video session available for purchase at ***TyndaleChristianResources.com****.*

A word in favor of the corporeal act of walking seems fitting here as we step into our second week, where the road to freedom rolls out for a captive Israel. We said from the start of this study that walking with God doesn't require feet. All it requires is response. We have a Maker who loves us, desires to both accompany us and savor our company, and invites us to move through the course of our lives in his rich fellowship.

For those physically able to take frequent walks or, if in a chair with wheels, frequent *rolls* out in the open air, the benefits to the heart, soul, mind, and body are well proven medically, scientifically, therapeutically, and—to individuals who make a habit of it—experientially. But what about spiritually? As we explore the theology of walking with God, let it be said that sometimes what we need most is to throw our physical body into it.

If walking isn't feasible, perhaps we could sit outside or throw open a window and prop our feet on the windowsill. Hear birds sing. Watch squirrels scamper up a tree. Feel a breeze against our faces. Scoot into a stream of sunshine and soak up some vitamin D. If you live in a busy neighborhood, you still have a sky above you and life teeming around you. Watch cars go by. Say hey to some neighbors. Get outside and out of your own head. We all hit a wall sometimes, slamming into the sudden end of our patience, creativity, energy, and good cheer. What's the best thing to do after we crash into a wall? Stumble someplace without one.

Routinely taking walks does more for my peace of mind than a hundred books on tranquility could. I can set out frustrated, agitated, or angry, pounding the ground, huffing rapidly, then by the time one mile turns to two, I'm often slowing down, breathing deeper, turning my thoughts northward, and trying to match the song I'm hearing from a nearby branch to the species of bird singing it. I took up the practice of daily strolling long before Keith and I moved to the country. I paced the streets near our city home, dodging Chevy pickups and petting the neighbors' dogs. Had my loved ones known what I worked out on those jaunts and how they changed my mood, they would have thanked God I went.

I bring up the value of the practice so that, in all this talking about walking with God, we don't make the concept so metaphorical we completely overlook the physical. Until our final gasp of air, our bodies and souls are inextricably connected. Our entire being is involved in worship, in work, in love (often the hardest work of all) in the angst of fought-for faith, in rest, in sleeping, in dreaming, and at play. And, anyway, the physical body is a marvel, don't you think? These skeletons, their ligaments and joints, these vital organs functioning without our having to tell them to, the blood coursing through our capillaries, the cells multiplying madly, these nerve endings telling us we're too close to a fire, these mysterious brains keeping it all straight, and this porous skin wrapping it all up in one piece? It's all rather extraordinary.

I didn't engage in daily gratitude to God for my body until it began to ache, weaken, and break with years of wear and tear. My appreciation for how God has used it to serve me awakened when it began to demand attention. These days when I set out on a walk—an act that invariably causes something to ache—I regularly say aloud to him, "Lord, thank you for my body. Sustain it and strengthen it again today." But if your body isn't aching yet, I hope you won't wait till it is. Start trying it now. Gratitude can wholly transform our body image, and in this brutal culture, such is a grace indeed. Your body is a beautiful, beautiful thing. Your Maker's masterpiece.

If the industrial revolution sent outside-oriented humans mostly inside, the technology that brought us screens and computers shut the doors and clicked the locks. We dwell in remarkable contrast with the ancient world, as much of our work, entertainment, and food preparation and consumption take place indoors. But these differences make the discussion more relevant rather than less, don't you think? We're privileged to be among the world's population with shelter from blistering heat and bone-chilling cold. But are we otherwise better off closed up and in? I don't think so. I don't think our lungs were fashioned to live with so little fresh air.

The change of perspective that can come with getting outside jumps to my attention every time I come upon Genesis 15, when the Lord appears to Abram in a vision announcing to him how great his reward will be. Abram's first response is to complain. "Look, you have given me no offspring, so a slave born in my house will be my heir" (Genesis 15:3). God reassures him an heir will come from his own body, but then God does something marvelous to make the point memorable.

> [The Lord] took him outside and said, "Look at the sky and count the stars, if you are able to count them. . . . Your offspring will be that numerous."
>
> GENESIS 15:5

Have you ever noticed our human propensity to close ourselves in with our disappointments and disillusionments until the air grows stale with discontent? We start ruminating on what or who didn't come through for us. Our problems and offenses get blown out of proportion, and the world shrinks to the circumference of our heads. Is it possible we also need God to take us outside in the fresh air under an expansive sky, where we can behold a universe that long preceded us and will long outlast us? Though we are treasured by the Lord and never insignificant, we are each one little sliver of a big, magnificent story. You'll see this in the interview with Makoto Fujimura this week.

We're about to watch a similar dynamic with the Israelites in the wilderness, where God makes the ground their escape and the starry sky their ceiling. Though God has them build a movable tent for his dwelling, stay alert to all the ways he meets them outside. You'll find that, when he provides them with sustenance, he doesn't bring it into their tents on a tray. He has them walk out and gather it up. He doesn't supply their rooms with tap water. He has them drink bubbling water from a rock.

NOTES

DAY 1

Moses replied, "We will go with our young and with our old; we will go with our sons and with our daughters, with our flocks and with our herds because we must hold the LORD's festival."

EXODUS 10:9

If I were your enemy, I'd magnify your fears, making them appear insurmountable, intimidating you with enough worries until avoiding them becomes your driving motivation. I would use anxiety to cripple you, to paralyze you, leaving you indecisive, clinging to safety and sameness, always on the defensive because of what might happen. When you hear the word faith, all I'd want you to hear is "unnecessary risk."

PRISCILLA SHIRER, *FERVENT*

In video session 2, we stood on the stepping stone for our second week's emphasis on walking with God, gazing at the remarkable promise he made to the Israelites in Leviticus 26:11-13. I'm including the segment again so we won't miss how the phrase "walked with God" in reference to Enoch and Noah is largely supplanted in this era by God saying, "I will walk among you." Can you hear the faintest echo of God walking among Adam and Eve in the garden? God is now taking the Israelites to a place that could hardly be further removed from Eden, but in his mercy, he is coming to join them.

I will place my residence among you, and I will not reject you. I will walk among you and be your God, and you will be my people. I am the LORD your God, who brought you out of the land of Egypt, so that you would no longer be their slaves. I broke the bars of your yoke and enabled you to live in freedom.

LEVITICUS 26:11-13

We'll spend all five days of this second week moving with the Israelites into and through the wilderness, where they receive the law of Moses, and as far removed as our lives may be, we find a wealth of opportunities we can relate to. Our frequent references to wilderness seasons in conversations of faith originate here in the forty tumultuous years the people of God spent between the exodus from Egypt and the conquest of Canaan. Never imagine that *in between* means *insignificant*. On God's atlas, the line doesn't just connect the dots. It often proves to balance the dots.

Flip through Exodus chapters 5–13, the narrative taking place in Egypt before the departure of the Israelites, noting the chapter headings. Pause at Exodus 7:16; 8:1, 20; 9:1, 13, and note the repetitions. What do all these scenes entail?

Now widen the lens on the next scene, which places Moses and Aaron before Pharaoh, and read Exodus 10:1-12. We see the same repetitions found in the verses above, but this time, note Pharaoh's fascinating concession. With the landscape freshly torn and tattered by the hailstorm, he is by no means anxious to welcome locusts, so he decides to negotiate. **Who did Pharaoh offer to release to go with Moses while they held this festival?**

Try to crawl into the head of Pharaoh for a moment. **What are a few reasons you imagine he offered to temporarily release the able-bodied men but not the women and children?** We're not given the reasons in Scripture, so feel free to explore several possibilities you find plausible.

Enjoy Moses's reply in Exodus 10:9: "We will go with our young and with our old; we will go with our sons and with our daughters, with our flocks and with our herds . . ." Savor the glorious inclusion of every segment of the community. God could have just summoned the young and left the old to die there. After all, think how many cultures see their elderly populations as disposable liabilities. He could also have said "men only," as he did on select occasions elsewhere. Instead, God called for the young and the old among his people, the men and the women. I'm reminded of a later time in the history of the Israelites when they were again in captivity and God spoke through the prophet Joel concerning the consummate deliverance of his people.

After this
I will pour out my Spirit on all humanity;
then your sons and your daughters will prophesy,
your old men will have dreams,
and your young men will see visions.
I will even pour out my Spirit
on the male and female slaves in those days.

JOEL 2:28-29

Sons and daughters. Old and young. Slaves, male and female.

Glance back to Exodus 10:10-11 and watch how Pharaoh reacts to Moses' insistence that none of the Israelites or their flocks and herds would be left behind. This commentary excerpt by Dr. John I. Durham may be a little hard to follow if you're new to certain terms, but the wordplay is too rich to miss. I'll expound somewhat after you read it.

> Moses' firmness serves, however, to confirm Pharaoh's suspicions, in actuality quite accurate ones, that the "pilgrimage" is really a flight. Thus does he rail out, in a sarcastic and quite clever word-play on the meaning of the tetragrammaton,

Divine tasks of faith are not about who we are but about who he is.

"'Yahweh' will indeed *be* with you when I fall for such a request as that!" Not yet has Pharaoh come to believe that any "One who always Is" can at last get the best of him, a point which this arrogant play on the name Yahweh makes with brilliant deftness.[1]

After God called out to Moses from the burning bush in Exodus 3–4 and informed him what he was going to do, he found, as in his foreknowledge he knew he would, a most unwilling party.

"Who am I?" (Exodus 3:11).
"They won't trust me" (Exodus 4:1).
"I am heavy of lip and thick of tongue" (Exodus 4:10).[2]

I can think of a myriad of reasons why I'm a poor choice for God to use. You too? I have often thought God either has a wealth of grace or decidedly poor taste. After all, who are we? But, you see, God would have us know that divine tasks of faith are not about who we are but about who he is. Impressively, Moses comes up with the right question.

If I go to the Israelites and say to them, "The God of
your ancestors has sent me to you," and they ask me,
"What is his name?" what should I tell them?
EXODUS 3:13

Fill in the following blanks to record God's full response to Moses in Exodus 3:14-15.

God replied to Moses, "______________________________
_________. This is what you are to say to the Israelites: I AM has sent me to you." God also said to Moses, "Say this to the Israelites: The ________________, the God of your ancestors, the God of Abraham, the God of Isaac, and the God of Jacob, has sent me to you. This is my name ____________________; this is how I am to be remembered in every generation."

When you filled in the second blank, did you happen to use all uppercase letters, as most formal translations of the Bible do in this verse, with the *L* a bit larger than "ORD"? If not, mark a line through it and write it exactly this way: LORD. In reference to the Divine, this is the tetragrammaton, a word comprised of four Hebrew letters we transliterate as *YHWH* or *YHVH*. God is called by many names in the Bible—Creator, King, Almighty, the Most High, Healer, Provider, and so forth—but when you see the word *LORD* in all uppercase letters, with the *L* a bit larger than "ORD," it represents the covenant name of God by which he introduced himself to Moses and the Israelites. Are you following?

Take a quick look at Psalm 8:1 for a perfect juxtaposition. Fill in the following blanks, printing the names exactly as you find them in the verse.

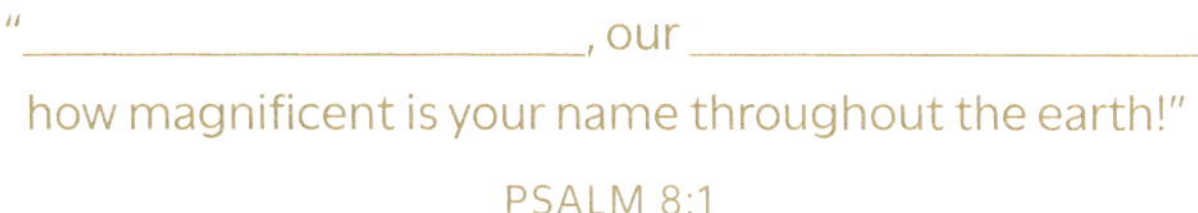

"____________________, our ____________________,
how magnificent is your name throughout the earth!"

PSALM 8:1

The first title, in all uppercase, translates the Hebrew *YHWH*. The second reference appears with the more standard uppercase *L* and lowercase *ord*. "Lord" here translates the Hebrew *Adonai*, meaning ruler or governor.

Let's get some insight on the meaning of "the LORD" from the same scholar we heard from earlier. Underline all the parts you find most fascinating or meaningful.

> "I AM that I AM," replies God. The verbs are first person common qal imperfects of the verb היה "to be," connoting continuing, unfinished action: "I am being that I am being," or "I am the Is-ing One," that is, "the One Who Always Is." Not conceptual being, being in the abstract, but active being, is the intent of this reply.[3]

Isn't "I am the Is-ing One" a marvelous way to imagine God introducing himself? Early on in my Bible study training, I heard "I AM that I AM" interpreted as "I Am Presently Happening." Each of these lends a bit of insight, inevitably limited, into the remarkable name by which God wants to be remembered throughout all generations.

Egypt's Pharaoh has a fiery reaction in Exodus 10:10 to Moses' insistence that all the Israelites would depart to worship God. His words, meant to be a threat, are an inadvertent declaration that this LORD (notice that Pharaoh uses the tetragrammaton) will have "to be" with Moses if he (Pharaoh) ever lets them go.

Both the Old Testament—inspired in Hebrew and some Aramaic—and the New Testament—inspired in Greek—are bulging at the seams with wordplay that often isn't obvious in our English translations. No two languages translate perfectly, so we often have to do a little extra work to appreciate them, but the more we're willing, the more fun it becomes.

Remember when you looked up Exodus 7:16; 8:1, 20; and 9:1, 13 for repetition? **Look back at one of these passages and complete this statement made by God and delivered to Pharaoh through Moses:**

Let my people go, that they ____________________

____________________________________.

Our focus these five weeks is on walking with God. The aspect we're highlighting throughout our second week is "The Law of Walking." We're peering into the Books of the Law to see how God was teaching the teachable to walk *with* him by walking *among* them.

When it comes to life with God, to be a walker is to be a worshiper.

When it comes to life with God, to be a walker is to be a worshiper. Worship is hemoglobin in the bloodstream of the one who walks with God, delivering the oxygen of the Holy Spirit to the tissues of the body. It keeps us going at times when nothing else will. If you're new to the concept, you'll be relieved to know worship doesn't just look one way in Scripture. A host of expressions color the pages, some of which we'll see in our next week of study. We mention it now, however briefly, because God hammered the point to Pharaoh. *Let my people go,* God said through Moses over and over, *that they may worship me.*

Two plagues later, Pharaoh let them go, but at the inestimable price of his and every other firstborn son among the Egyptians. Though Pharoah and his overlords had enslaved the Israelites and burdened them beyond all human capacity, ignoring their cries, it's chilling to imagine the outbreak of grief at that time.

> During the night Pharaoh got up, he along with all his officials and all the Egyptians, and there was a loud wailing throughout Egypt because there wasn't a house without someone dead. He summoned Moses and Aaron during the night and said, "Get out immediately from among my people, both you and the Israelites, and go, worship the LORD as you have said. Take even your flocks and your herds as you asked and leave, and also bless me."
>
> Now the Egyptians pressured the people in order to send them quickly out of the country, for they said, "We're all going to die!"
>
> EXODUS 12:30-33

Ever notice how an explosive crisis can make us yell "Get out!" before we really mean it? The footprints of the departed Israelites were still pressed in the sands of Goshen when Pharaoh reconsidered what he'd done. The great heights of his acclaimed kingdom were built on the backs of slaves. The sun rose the next morning on unlaid bricks and silent hammers. Who'd do the work? The Egyptians? They'd have to be paid! This, you see, would never do. He'd been temporarily blinded by grief, but his greed tumbled him back to his senses.

> [Pharaoh] got his chariot ready and took his troops with him; he took six hundred of the best chariots and all the rest of the chariots of Egypt, with officers in each one. . . . The Egyptians—all Pharaoh's horses and chariots, his horsemen, and his army—chased after them and caught up with them as they camped by the sea."
>
> EXODUS 14:6-7, 9

Exodus 14:10 paints the Israelites in a most precarious position, sandwiched between the Red Sea and the Egyptian army in a fury, come to reclaim their slaves. Only one thing is worse than being pinned in, and that's packed in. Imagine the viral panic, the urge to stampede but with nowhere to go.

Read Exodus 14:10-12. In a nutshell, what did the Israelites say to Moses?

Compare Exodus 14:13-14. What did Moses tell them to do?

Stay alert, because this part is important. **What, on the contrary, did the Lord tell Moses to say to the people in Exodus 14:15?**

Did you catch the distinctions among the three responses to the crisis?

- The Israelites: "We should have stayed in Egypt!"
- Moses: "No, no, don't wish you could go back! Just stand still, and God will fight for you!"
- God: "Why do you cry to me? Tell the people of Israel to go forward!"

Sound familiar? Aren't those the same three options we often face? We know we need to do something fast, but *what?*

- Go back!
- Stand still!
- Go forward!

Which direction has most strongly pulled at you recently, and why?

We've discussed how the concept of walking with God communicates movement. Moments do arise when God instructs us, as the angel of the Lord instructed Hagar in Genesis 16:9, to "go back." We also run into situations when God tells us to stay put and stand tight. But God's favorite action verb at the most pivotal junctures in Scripture is undoubtedly "Go!" (Genesis 12:1; Matthew 2:20; Matthew 28:19; John 14:2.) God is ever moving us onward, "from glory to glory" (2 Corinthians 3:18) and "from strength to strength" until "each appears before God in Zion" (Psalm 84:7).

Even when he directs us to go back or stand still, it is invariably toward the goal of going forward. This I can promise you about your walk with God: The direction he wants you facing is forward. Your future is not like your past. The person you were is not the person you're becoming. In the divine agenda, any going back, any standing still is ultimately about going forward.

If God says "Go!" but the way ahead is blocked, as it was for the Israelites, it's up to God to make a way for you to obey. In their case, he parted the sea with vigorous gales, heaping its foamy edges into walls of water, and the people crossed on dry ground. Our openings may not be nearly as dramatic; nevertheless, when the way ahead opens, we need not form a committee to pray about it. We need to get up and move.

Stay light on your feet, pilgrim.

DAY 2

LORD, who is like you among the gods? Who is like you, glorious in holiness, revered with praises, performing wonders?

EXODUS 15:11

What if it's the there
and not the here
that I long for?
The wander
and not the wait,
the magic
in the lost feet
stumbling down
the faraway street
and the way the moon
never hangs
quite the same.

TYLER KNOTT GREGSON, *CHASERS OF THE LIGHT*

Today we officially enter Israel's wilderness (or *midbar*) season, an era initiated with a rousing song. We could easily spend our whole lesson on this solitary song, but since we have substantial ground to cover in "The Law of Walking," I'll include a bit of background, then hasten to point out something sublime. **Peruse Exodus 15:1-18. What specific event inspired the song?**

Perhaps you'll find scholar Douglas K. Stuart's dating of this song or psalm as fascinating as I did.

> This "Song of the Sea" probably was the earliest-authored portion of the book of Exodus. Moses apparently composed it immediately after the deliverance that it describes (15:1), and Miriam, Moses' sister, taught it forthwith to the women of Israel (15:20-21).[4]

This ode to victory begins with the words "I will sing to the LORD." Appreciate the determination: "I *will* sing. My God has been too faithful for me not to sing." **Have you ever determined you were going to sing to the Lord no matter what and no matter how you sounded, simply because he is worthy? What occasion stands out most in your memory?**

What happens in Exodus 15:20-21?

Remember how the Israelites were to approach the meal that first Passover? "Here is how you must eat it," Exodus 12:11 reads. "You must be dressed for travel, your sandals on your feet, and your staff in your hand. You are to eat it in a hurry; it is the LORD's Passover."

Be ready to go!

The Israelite women are hurriedly packing the necessities for life on the go. Imagine being among them and murmuring to yourself, "Okay, let's see. What am I missing? Oh, my tambourine!" The tambourines could conceivably have been among the items the Egyptian women sent with them, but the fact the Israelite women knew exactly how to file out in an ancient line dance with Miriam, timbrels in hand, indicates they knew how to use them.

Here's what I'd like to kick my heels up about: Faith packs a tambourine. Faith says, "We may not know where we're going, but we know the same God who has delivered us will be good to us." What could be more relevant in a long walk with God than learning to anticipate reasons in every season to worship? Faith includes praise in all its travel plans.

We will use the words *wilderness* and *desert* interchangeably this week, as Scripture often does, in translation of the Hebrew term *midbar* (מִדְבָּר). Not in Egypt nor in Canaan did God promise to walk among the Israelites and make them his people; rather, there in the wildly unwelcoming *midbar* he stepped into their ranks.

Faith packs a tambourine.

If you have mixed feelings about the wilderness as a biblical motif, you're in good company. No one wants to go to the desert with God, but once a person has been there, it's impossible to imagine a rich spiritual journey without it. It's a complicated place on divine purpose. **Record how the wilderness is described in the following passages:**

Deuteronomy 1:19

Deuteronomy 8:15

To be sure, the land the Israelites traversed was every bit wilderness, but the glorious aspect about any weary land God occupies with his children is how he appears to find bleak scenes the perfect backdrop for artful wonders.

Read Deuteronomy 8:15-16, and this time record some of the wonders God's people experienced.

This is the desert paradox. The cactus flower, so to speak. There in the howling wilderness, something holy happens. Not always visibly, of course. And not always right away. The wilderness isn't meant to be conflated with grief, but when it is the driving force of a desert season, grief can be so thorough, so utterly complete, that not the faintest flicker of light can be discerned. In the words of the psalmist emanating from a dry well of despair, "Darkness is my only friend" (Psalm 88:18).

We do our loved ones no favors, nor they us, when we suggest they look on the bright side of a pitch-dark hole. Sometimes there is no bright side. There is only darkness. I know a couple whose three young sons—all the children they had—were murdered by an escaped convict. We can strike all the matches in our spiritual arsenals and still not light up the face of Jesus for someone in such a depth of despair. He alone can make himself known. And he will, in time, when they can take it. Till then, he's there in the black hole with them, closer than air, fellowshipping with them—I have to believe *weeping* with them—in their grief.

Thankfully, our wilderness seasons typically lean more toward desperation than abject despair. They may closely parallel the desperation the ancient Israelites felt on the long road from Egypt to Canaan. We may feel lost and isolated like they did, scared of what we can't see and stung by what we can. Our comforts elude us. Our tasks bore us. Our obstacles defy us. Our enemies—both real and imagined—haunt us. Little, if anything, is recognizable. We feel like we're wandering in circles. Like we've lost our way. Or like our Way has lost us.

> **We feel like we're wandering in circles. Like we've lost our way. Or like our Way has lost us.**

He hasn't.

But, if we have eyes to see—oh, the wonders God does in the wilderness. How he feeds us on his words. Carries us in his arms. Favors us. Woos us. Speaks over us. Reveals himself to us. **Have you ever experienced this phenomenon? If so, describe a wilderness season of your own when life was so hard but God seemed particularly unabashed in his goodness.**

When I was forty years old, God escorted me into a wilderness season that, to this day, still causes me to wince in remembrance. Within a very short period, a little boy who'd been in our home and part of our lives for seven years went back to his mom, a relationship fractured beyond repair, my mother died of breast cancer, and my firstborn went away to college. I felt like I'd been skinned and every nerve ending in my body left exposed. Physical pain throbbed in my chest as if a knife were lodged between two ribs.

I was so desperate for hope from God, my face stayed pressed to the sacred pages. Even the most familiar passages read like drops of water on my parched tongue. I sang worship songs like my life depended on them being true. Depended on Jesus being worthy. And they were true, and he is worthy.

Dependence. This is what makes the desert cactus bloom. Without it, all is thorns and bitterness. Wonders are not guaranteed in a wilderness. When they come, they are graces availed to those humbled enough by need to rely entirely on God.

Months later, as I knelt on the ground watering some early summer flowers I'd planted, I suddenly realized that the pain in my chest was gone and I didn't feel so much like crying and the sun was warm on my shoulders and the soil gentle under my knees. I said to the Lord aloud, "It's over, isn't it?" And I wept.

I wept with gratitude, of course, because nothing is romantic about pain, and the many months prior had been racked with it. But I also wept because it wasn't just that the desperation and pain were on pause but also that it had been a season thick with wonder. I'm not saying this is how it has to be. God can do whatever he pleases. But I'm suggesting this often seems to be the case, and wouldn't we want it to be this way? At the end of the day, don't we want a God so merciful he'd reserve the right to favor those who ache? I'm never more taken with Jesus than when I picture him delivering the Sermon on the Mount and saying things like this:

> Blessed are those who mourn, for they will be comforted.
>
> MATTHEW 5:4

Blessed are you when you need me, for you shall have me! Isn't that what he seems to be saying? That God has at times broken through our hard shell of comfortlessness—our *Don't touch me! Leave me alone!*—with comfort. This is itself a wonder, don't you think? The problem with miracles is how seldom we get one when we don't need one. When we're walking through a desert season, the elements and even the individuals around us are notorious for not coming through in our need. But the beauty of the wilderness is that in our lack, if we're willing, we can cry out and, in time, there he comes—invisible yet unmistakable.

For the Israelites in that original wilderness season, wonders were seen, not just sensed with enlightened eyes of the heart, and not remotely left to the imagination. Their most constant Presence-reflecting provision from God came in the form of manna.

Please read Exodus 16:4-35, and answer the following questions. What did the manna look like?

(Enjoy how Numbers 11:7 says the appearance of the manna "was like that of bdellium," as if we current readers are going to say, "Oh, bdellium! That explains it!")

What did it taste like?

How often were the Israelites to gather it?

In your understanding based on this text alone, what are a few reasons God required a Sabbath, even as it related to the manna?

According to the timing given in Exodus 16:1, God started raining this bread from heaven on the Israelites about a month after they left Egypt. The provisions they'd taken on the journey had likely carried them until now. God undoubtedly wanted them to face their own limitations to provide and then ask for his help. What he could have done without was the grumbling and complaining and the deceitful romanticizing of Egypt.

Delightfully, the word *manna* means "What is it?" The children of Israel could complain about the unfamiliarity and lack of variety if they wanted to, but they couldn't deny the miracle of the manna. Their lives literally depended on it. Most of us can say we haven't often seen creative miracles undeniable to an entire congregation. In human (as opposed to biblical) usage, the term *miracle* can be relative. What seems miraculous to me might not seem wondrous to you at all, and the same might be true in reverse. **Can you think of a time when you tried to tell another believer what a miraculous thing God had done for you but the person clearly didn't get it? How might you explain the differing outlooks?**

Different outlooks get even more interesting when they come from the same singular set of eyes. What seemed miraculous to us at the time it occurred, for instance, might not seem as much so in retrospect. The reverse can also be true. We might not conclude God intervened supernaturally until years later. So which outlook was accurate? For most of us, our journeys with God stretch out over many miles and years. Our faith ebbs and flows. Our understanding dims and grows. We're more sensitive to the Holy Spirit some days. We can also let our imaginations get away from us. We go through seasons awhirl with yeses from God. Just when we're about to package a formula for how to get what we want from God, heaven seems to go silent. All these things are normative in a long walk with God. We won't figure it all out. We won't deduce it all correctly. Won't exegete it all accurately. But we can appreciate it all deeply.

That's what I want to say in these pages, from a testimonial standpoint as much as anything else. Appreciate all of it. A walk with God involves it all.

Let's not get so sophisticated that we start feeling silly for what seemed extraordinary to us at a different point in our walk. Don't belittle the God of your youth or look down on the ways he sought to delight you. Believe me when I say you will desperately need him to do likewise in your older age. Don't cringe when you reflect on a testimony you gave earlier in your walk. God no more despised us in our growing process than a parent despises an infant for not knowing how to walk. If it was a good gift and it made you feel known and loved by God, it came from a miracle-working God, whether it was a miracle or not. Above all, let us not lose our faith. If in our pursuit of deeper biblical knowledge God gets smaller and weaker, we are not growing up. We are growing cold.

DAY 3

I led you forty years in the wilderness; your clothes and the sandals on your feet did not wear out.

DEUTERONOMY 29:5

Everybody ends up somewhere in life. Decide to end up somewhere on purpose.

ANDY STANLEY

I'd like to begin day 3 with encouragement to those who are new to the study of Scripture through some common experiences of those who have been at it for years. From countless conversations with women over the course of forty years, this is what seems to have been true for many of us.

Some of us began Bible study because we were Christians and rightly wanted to know more about God and do his will. Others weren't Christians yet. They were simply invited to a neighbor's home and took the chance, or had a life crisis and someone suggested Bible study could really help. What I believe I can say for most of us who never stopped is that what began as a right thing to do developed into what we longed to do. Obligation—not a bad thing, mind you—developed into affection.

A number of us who developed a lasting love of studying Scripture would say something in particular clicked with us, capturing our imagination or attention and swinging our hearts wide open. It might have been a sermon series at church. It might have been a study on one of the Gospels in a small group that suddenly brought the whole Bible to life. It might have

Obligation can develop into affection.

been a topical study, like one on marriage, parenting, spiritual gifts, or eschatology. For me, it was the study of the Old Testament Tabernacle.

It was accidental, really. I was in my very early thirties, reading through Exodus in my own devotional time, and I got to the twenty-fifth chapter, the eighth and ninth verses, where the Lord was speaking to Moses.

> They are to make a sanctuary for me so that I may dwell among them. You must make it according to all that I show you—the pattern of the tabernacle as well as the pattern of all its furnishings.

I couldn't recall having heard much of anything about the Old Testament Tabernacle in three decades of church and then came to find some fifty chapters of Scripture devoted to it. I kept asking myself, *Where has this been?* This ancient tent caught me in its portable walls and kept me for months, poring over Scripture, discovering a world of connections between the Old and New Testaments. My head spun over what the former foreshadowed and the latter fulfilled.

I share this previous story in preparation for an assignment I'm asking you to complete before the end of this week. Below you'll find two columns, along with space at the top of each to fill in a name. Contact two accessible people you know who have loved the study of Scripture for ten or more years and ask what caught or captured them. You can easily do this by text. The responses need not be dramatic nor support my suggestion that, for many, something suddenly clicked. **Just ask them what originally captured them, then return to these two columns and record the individual's name and reply.**

Name ______________________	Name ______________________

The Israelites did as God instructed them and built the ornate portable Tabernacle (or "tent of testimony") and all its furnishings, precisely according to the pattern he gave them. Just as he promised, God blessed it with his glorious and holy presence. This ushers us to our text for today. **Please read Numbers 9:15-23.**

How did God manifest his accompanying presence once the Tabernacle was set up?

Was the cloud static or dynamic?

How exactly did God use this manifestation of his divine presence to guide the Israelites' journey?

Fill in the following blanks, according to Numbers 9:18.

At the LORD's command ______________________,
and at the LORD's command ______________________.

Look carefully at Numbers 9:15-23. How many times are the previous words said in the segment?

Imagine how refreshing these acts of obedience must have been to God!

Glance back at Numbers 9:19. Scholar Timothy R. Ashley's more literal translation of "carried out the LORD's requirement" is captivating: The Israelites "kept the watch of Yahweh." "The expression *kept the watch of Yahweh*, when connected with the sanctuary or the Levites, means 'guard duty.'"[5] They didn't just wait. They watched for the Lord to move.

Read Numbers 9:21. Can you imagine? Sometimes the Israelites would barely make camp only to break camp. Which do you think would have been most challenging for you psychologically: the cloud moving just about the time the Tabernacle was set up in the new location or the cloud lingering for days on end and not knowing when to expect to advance on the journey? **Explain your answer.**

Rabbinic Hebrew came to reference God's resident presence as *shekinah*. "Although the word 'Shekinah' does not occur in the Bible, the root *škn* occurs not only in the verb ('dwell'), but also in the noun *miškān* ('dwelling place,' 'tabernacle')."[6]

Read the following definition of the word *shekinah* carefully. Underline the sentence that includes the word *tabernacle* so you'll remember it.

> **Shekinah** (she-kī'nuh), a Hebrew word from the root "to dwell" that is translated as the "Presence" of God. . . . Rabbinic literature refers to God's *Shekinah* in a variety of contexts. God's presence was seen in the cloud that led the Israelites in the desert and in the tent of meeting in the desert. The Priestly writer's word for the tent of meeting, the *mishkan* or "tabernacle," comes from the same root as *Shekinah*. The glory of God, which filled the Temple, was his *Shekinah* and when the Temple was destroyed, God's *Shekinah* left the Temple.[7]

Whatever you do, don't doze off during this next part. **Read John 1:14-18. "The Word" (*Logos*) is in reference to Jesus. Having become flesh, what did "the Word" do, according to John 1:14?**

In the same verse, what did they observe?

Now read this insight into John 1:14, and star every word or concept it has in common with the earlier definition of *shekinah*.

> The Gr. word for tent (tabernacle) is the root (*skēnē*) of a NT verb, *skēnoō*, describing the purpose of the life of Christ: like the tabernacle, He is the residence and manifestation of God's presence and glory among His people ("And the Word became flesh and tabernacled among us") (Jn 1:14, NASB).[8]

Look back at the previous sentence and fill in this blank accordingly:

"The Word became flesh and ______________________ among us."

To remove any lingering skepticism about the connections between the Old Testament Tabernacle and John 1:14-16, read this commentary excerpt by Dr. George R. Beasley-Murray.

> The language is evocative of the revelation of God's glory in the Exodus—by the Red Sea, on Mount Sinai, and at the tent of meeting by Israel's camp (especially the last; see Exod 33:7-11; for the glory in and upon the Tabernacle cf. Exod 40:34-38).
>
> The Exodus associations are intentional, and are part of the theme of the revelation and redemption of the Logos-Christ as fulfilling the hope of a *second* Exodus.[9]

A second Exodus. Isn't that spectacular? John 1 opens with a deliberate echo of the creation narrative in Genesis 1 and transitions magnificently at verse 14 into a reverberation of Exodus. Behold the brilliance of the Scriptures.

Remember, consistency is among the most self-authenticating qualities of divine inspiration. In both Testaments, clouds are frequently included in descriptions of God's manifest presence. Intriguingly, God used cloud covering in large part as a mercy to protect the people from himself. The Israelites—and we, for that matter—could not survive an unfiltered view of the divine glory. You may recall the Lord's words to Moses in Exodus 33:20: "You cannot see my face, for humans cannot see me and live."

What follows is a mere sampling of verses that mention clouds in close proximity to God, particularly in reference to a divine manifestation of some kind. **Fill in each blank with the word *cloud*, and underline any part of the verse stating or suggesting the cloud's purpose. Lastly, circle the reference so you can track the breadth of history they cover.** The first six verses are selected from different books in the Old Testament.

> The LORD said to Moses, "I am going to come to you in a
> dense ____________________, so that the people will
> hear when I speak with you and will always believe you."
> Moses reported the people's words to the LORD.
>
> EXODUS 19:9

(Note: This is one of nineteen references to a cloud representing God's presence in Exodus.)

> Then the LORD descended in the ____________________ and
> spoke to him. He took some of the Spirit who was on Moses
> and placed the Spirit on the seventy elders. As the Spirit rested
> on them, they prophesied, but they never did it again.
>
> NUMBERS 11:25

(Note: This is one of sixteen similar references in Numbers.)

> He obscures the view of his throne, spreading
> his ____________________ over it.
>
> JOB 26:9

> ____________________s and total darkness surround him;
> righteousness and justice are the foundation of his throne.
>
> PSALM 97:2

> I looked, and there was a whirlwind coming from the north, a
> huge ______________ with fire flashing back and forth and brilliant
> light all around it. In the center of the fire, there was a gleam like
> amber. . . . The appearance of the brilliant light all around was

like that of a rainbow in a ______________________ on a rainy
day. This was the appearance of the likeness of the LORD's glory.
When I saw it, I fell facedown and heard a voice speaking.

EZEKIEL 1:4, 28

I continued watching in the night visions, and suddenly one like a
son of man was coming with the ________________s of heaven. He
approached the Ancient of Days and was escorted before him.

DANIEL 7:13

Now we cross from the Old Testament to the New Testament with a few among many references.

While he was still speaking, suddenly a bright
_______________________ covered them, and a voice from
the ______________________ said, "This is my beloved
Son, with whom I am well-pleased. Listen to him!"

MATTHEW 17:5

The sign of the Son of Man will appear in the sky, and
then all the peoples of the earth will mourn; and they will
see the Son of Man coming on the ________________s
of heaven with power and great glory.

MATTHEW 24:30

"You have said it," Jesus told him. "But I tell you, in the future
you will see the Son of Man seated at the right hand of Power
and coming on the ____________________s of heaven."

MATTHEW 26:64

The context of this verse is Christ's ascension:

After he had said this, he was taken up as they were watching,
and a ______________________ took him out of their sight.

ACTS 1:9

The context of this verse is Christ's second advent:

> Look, he is coming with the ____________________s, and every eye will see him, even those who pierced him. And all the tribes of the earth will mourn over him. So it is to be. Amen.
>
> REVELATION 1:7

Record any observations you can make based on the preceding verses.

A thought as we wrap up today's lesson: Perhaps, like me, you wish you had a visible cloud by day and fire by night through which God directed you to stay or leave. Like me, you may often wish Jesus would appear right before your eyes and say the words aloud, as he did in the Gospels. We have neither advantage in this age, but what we do have that our predecessors did not is the completed canon. We who are in Christ also have the indwelling Holy Spirit, by whom we are led. We'll discuss more about what that looks like when we reach our final week of *Walking with God*. For now, however, the cloudy pillar offers some imagery worth contemplating in our own journey.

We get antsy, ill at ease, disappointed, or bored at times where we are and where, to the best of our understanding, we believe God brought us. We can't figure out if God is calling us to go elsewhere or to push through unease right where we are. Sometimes the circumstances make this kind of direction clear-cut in Scripture, but often it's not. We pray for wisdom and discernment from the Lord and seek godly advice. We may also receive a cue from the Holy Spirit, similar in concept to the cloudy pillar. This is subjective, of course, and by no means foolproof, but here's what I've experienced a handful of times in my adult life.

I'll start getting a sense in my spirit that my time in a particular place may be coming to an end. If I've been there long, I've inevitably formed relationships and assumed responsibilities, so my first instinct is to think I can't possibly leave. The sense that God wants me to let go and move on grows, and so does my resistance. *Lord, I love this place. I love these people. I don't want to leave. And I hate change.* Then his presence with me—not inside me, mind you, but with me or perhaps more pointedly, *on* me—seems to fade.

Case in point: I taught Bible study for years at a church to a group of people I could not have loved more. Inexplicably, God began to stir in me the sense that he was about to call me out.

I resisted. Everything I began to read in my morning devotionals increasingly screamed, *Go!* I said to the Lord, "Just one more Bible study, Lord. After all, they've already advertised for it. Let me just have this final one." I've never taught a study where I sensed the Lord's hand on me less. It was miserable. Staying that one more quarter was the wrong thing to do. I should have gone when he said and asked the church's forgiveness for not being able to do what I'd planned. In the imagery of the cloudy pillar, it seemed as if God were saying, *My presence where you are concerned is going. You can either go with me or stay here without me.*

I don't know if these kinds of subjective examples are helpful, but one thing I've come to deeply appreciate over the years is Moses' absolute insistence on being where God was. "If your presence does not go," Moses said to the Lord in Exodus 33:15, "don't make us go up from here." Likewise, "If your presence is going, Lord, do not make us stay."

On day 1 of this second week, we talked about occasions when God directs us to go back, stay where we are, or move ahead. Today's verses not only chime in on similar directions. The imagery of the cloudy pillar also preaches a sermon on pacing. When we are directed to move ahead, God doesn't just have a place for us to go. He has a pace for us to go. Pacing requires attentiveness to the Scriptures, to the things of the Spirit, and to prayer. We can get ahead of God and arrive before we're ready or go at a cautious snail's pace, and either way we miss an opportunity. Thankfully, we never outgrow God's parenting. He knows precisely how to train us to pay attention.

Thankfully, we never outgrow God's parenting.

DAY 4

Now if I have indeed found favor with you, please teach me your ways, and I will know you, so that I may find favor with you. Now consider that this nation is your people.

EXODUS 33:13

It's often said that God works in mysterious ways. You have to really think about what He's trying to do. You can't be lazy and believe in God; He doesn't make it that easy. It takes spirit and faith and passion to really believe.

DAVID BALDACCI, *THE CHRISTMAS TRAIN*

Our aim this week has been to investigate "The Law of Walking" to further develop our understanding of what is meant by walking with God. When we conclude this second week, we will have peered into all five Books of the Law. Week 1 was spent entirely in Genesis, then we launched week 2 in our video session about the book of Leviticus, establishing the twelfth verse of the twenty-sixth chapter as the driving force for the week:

I will walk among you and be your God, and you will be my people.

LEVITICUS 26:12

Days 1, 2, and 3 had us primarily in Exodus and Numbers, with a few glimpses into Deuteronomy. Our remaining two days will plant us more firmly into the rich soil of the fifth and final book of the Torah. The following has been our premise:

God walked *among* his people to teach his people how to walk *with* him.

Deuteronomy unfolds with Moses standing before a new generation of Israelites. Just as God promised, the faithless generation that had entered the wilderness died away, except Joshua and Caleb. They were the only two spies sent to scout out Canaan who believed the Israelites were completely capable of taking the land because God had given it to them. Caleb insisted,

> "Let's go up now and take possession of the land because we can certainly conquer it!" But the men who had gone up with him responded, "We can't attack the people because they are stronger than we are!"
>
> NUMBERS 13:30-31

The negative report caused panic to set in to the whole community, and they catastrophized what awaited them. *We'll die by the sword! They will take our wives and children as plunder! Imagine what they'll do to them!*

This unbelief was not a rare moment of panic. It characterized that generation of adults. **The Lord had a few words of his own to say in Numbers 14:30-34. Turn to this passage in your Bible so you can fill in the blanks.**

> I swear that none of you will enter the land I promised to settle you in, except Caleb son of Jephunneh and Joshua son of Nun. I will bring your children whom you said would become plunder into the land you rejected, and ______________________________ __________. But as for you, your corpses will fall in this wilderness. Your children will be shepherds in the wilderness for forty years and bear the penalty for your acts of unfaithfulness until all your corpses lie scattered in the wilderness. You will bear the consequences of your iniquities ______________________ based on the number of the ______________________ that you scouted the land, a year for each day. You will know my displeasure.
>
> NUMBERS 14:30-34

Now turn to Deuteronomy and read 1:1-3. What is the date Moses began this address to the Israelites?

These events are not just once upon a time. They happened on very real days of very real months in very real years of Israel's history. They are bold dots nailed down for keeps on the biblical timeline.

Moses' audience in Deuteronomy is comprised of the children of that generation, now in the full throes of adulthood, on the cusp of entering the land God promised they'd enjoy. He begins the address with a recent history lesson to remind them of the promises and wonders of God and the unfaithfulness of their parents' generation. Moses then reteaches them the law. The meaning of the word *Deuteronomy* is "second law," but rather than an entirely new set, think of it as the reiteration of the laws previously given (particularly in Exodus), with some additions.

Deuteronomy makes an enormous contribution to our theme because it includes multiple references to walking, and each appears in a blatantly theological context. Most of them appear in exhortations similar to what we find in Deuteronomy 8:6. **Take a look at this verse. How were the Israelites to keep the Lord's commands?**

- Deuteronomy 10:12 says it again: "Walking in all his ways."
- Deuteronomy 11:22, again: "Walk in all his ways."
- Deuteronomy 19:9, again: "Walking in his ways at all times."
- Deuteronomy 26:17; 28:9; 30:16, each yet again: "Walk in his ways."

The repetitive exhortation begs a question: So what are the Lord's ways? This is the inquiry that will hold our attention for the remainder of our lesson. You'll recall that Deuteronomy 8:6 specifically says that they keep the Lord's commands by walking in his ways. His commands were more than the Ten Commandments, but certainly not less. **Peruse Deuteronomy 5:6-21. If those are reflective of God's ways, what are a few ways you might describe him based solely on these commands?**

In Mark 12:28-31, a scribe asks Jesus which commandment is the most important of all. How does Jesus answer him?

Go now to the Ten Commandments in Exodus 20:1-17. Which of them seem to you to reflect ways of loving God?

How about loving neighbor?

Now go to Deuteronomy 10 and read verses 12-22. In verse 12, Moses tells the Israelites what God is asking of them.

> Now, Israel, what does the LORD your God ask of you except to fear the LORD your God by walking in all his ways, to love him, and to worship the LORD your God with all your heart and all your soul?

Remember, our present task is to try to determine what God's ways are like, since the Israelites were called to walk in them. **Search Deuteronomy 10:13-22 and list everything about God's ways that can be drawn from that immediate context.**

Now take a quick glance at the following segments that include instructions about how the Israelites were to live with one another in community. What were the ways of the Lord their God, based on each one?

Deuteronomy 4:41-42

Deuteronomy 15:1-2

Deuteronomy 15:7

Deuteronomy 15:12-15

Finally, what was God asking the Israelites to do in Deuteronomy 6:18 so they might prosper and possess the good land he promised?

If time permitted, we'd also find in the pages of Deuteronomy a God whose way it is to commemorate, feast, and celebrate in community. We'd find a God whose way it is to bless his people but also protect them from the ruination of pride by requiring that they remember with grateful hearts who brought them into that good land. And, yes, we'd find some commands that shake our sensibilities and mystify us, but these ancient laws made more sense in their time, place, and culture and certainly as they compared and contrasted to the laws of neighboring nations.

We will also soon see a Savior who satisfied the law completely, fulfilling every requirement.

Here is the question I'm posing as we draw this lesson to conclusion: Are the ways of this God of the Israelites and this God of ours worth emulating? Is this God even good? Are his ways right? Do his ways come from a supreme being with mixed motives or of pure holiness? You've seen in these glimpses of Deuteronomy a God who insists on justice, honesty, goodness to neighbor, generosity to the poor, kindness to the orphan and the widow, hospitality to the resident alien, faithfulness to spouse, respect for another's property. You've seen a God who insists on rest from labor and on untouchable cities of refuge for those who accidentally caused harm and who fear retribution. We find a God driven by love who chose a people to bless and be a blessing who'd done nothing to earn it.

When we get to the New Testament, we'll encounter this same God's one and only Son, who didn't just say, "Walk in my ways," but "I am the Way." And we will ask ourselves again: Is this a God worth following? Is this a way worth walking?

DAY 5

If anyone has ears to hear, let him listen.

MARK 4:23

The very moment you wake up each morning . . . all your wishes and hopes for the day rush at you like wild animals. And the first job each morning consists simply in shoving them all back; in listening to that other voice, taking that other point of view, letting that other larger, stronger, quieter life come flowing in.

C. S. LEWIS, *JOYFUL CHRISTIAN*

I can think of no better place to land our week's focus on "The Law of Walking" than in Deuteronomy 6:4-9. You'll quickly recognize how it pertains to our study. This paragraph in Scripture is begging to be handwritten and actively imagined. **Write all six verses in the space below, following these two instructions:**

- Note the appearance of the tetragrammaton LORD and copy it accordingly.
- Write the word *all* in uppercase letters (ALL) each time you come to it.

Next, follow these instructions:

- Comb through your handwritten verses and circle every instruction-oriented verb in the text. For example, begin by circling *listen* and *love*.
- Underline every appearance of the word *your*, along with the word immediately following it. For instance, your first underlined pairing is found in verse 5: *your God*.
- In very visual texts, even the simplest, least artistic illustrations can engage the imagination. Step into verses 6-9 as if you're acting them out, and hand-draw basic pictures illustrating the passage well enough to know at a glance what the verses instruct without looking at a single word. Several of the verses include more than one visual, so try not to skip any. Sketch all your drawings vertically so they appear down the page in order. I know, I know. You probably want to skip this exercise, but I promise it will have value. These verses were meant to come alive in the listener's imagination. Keep in mind that this isn't art class. This is Bible study.

Verse 6

Verse 7

Verse 8

Verse 9

Glance back at the work you've accomplished so far in this lesson, from writing the Scripture passage to underlining and circling to illustrating. When God gave these commands to Moses to preach to the Israelites at Canaan's edge, he meant for them to practice the words on their tongues and picture the images so they could see how they'd fit practically into their personal, familial, communal, lying-down, getting-up, going-out, coming-back lives.

Deuteronomy 6:4 in particular and 6:5-9 by extension comprise what is traditionally called the *Shema*. If this term is new to you, the first step is knowing how to pronounce it, since English speakers are inclined to accent the first syllable rather than the second. *Shema* is pronounced "shuh-MAH," or "sheh-MAH," as long as you don't overdo the *e*. The first syllable runs quickly into the second, with almost no vowel sound at all, then you slow down and take your time on the *ma*. No gutturals.

It's virtually impossible to overstate the significance of Shema in Jewish life over the years and centuries that followed Moses' sermon. The closest recited text we have in the Christian faith is the Lord's Prayer, and the frequency with which most of us say it pales in comparison. Because Deuteronomy 11:13-21 and Numbers 15:37-41 include similar concepts, they ultimately joined Deuteronomy 6:4-9 as the central affirmation and recitation of Judaism. Not only were the three paragraphs recited frequently in many Jewish services, they were also recited in the home twice daily—once in the morning and again in the evening. These deeply revered practices are still observed in synagogues and the homes of devout Jews.

Remember from yesterday's lesson how Jesus answered the scribe's question, "Teacher, which command in the law is the greatest?" Almost doubtlessly, the first segment of Scripture Jesus learned as a young child barely able to talk was the Shema.

Hearing first from a Jewish scholar on the Scriptures that are so foundational to Judaism will aid us immensely. In *The JPS Torah Commentary* on Deuteronomy, Dr. Jeffrey H. Tigay writes,

> The position of this paragraph in Deuteronomy lends it special significance. . . . It is, in a sense, the beginning of Deuteronomy proper. It concisely states the central themes of the book and the central demands of the covenant, paraphrasing the first commandment and explicating its meaning: Israel's love and loyalty to YHVH must be undivided and accompanied by constant efforts to remember His instructions and teach them to future generations. The significance of this paragraph is reflected in the fact that it became the centerpiece of Jewish daily worship, the *Keri'at Shema'* ("Recitation of the Shema"), named for the first word.[10]

What is the first word of Deuteronomy 6:4?

Depending on the Bible translation you're using, you likely filled the blank with the word *hear* (ESV, KJV, NASB, NIV) or *listen* (CSB). The word *shema* (Hebrew שְׁמַע) is vigorous enough in this context to also indicate synonyms like "Pay attention!" and "Focus!" The Complete Jewish Bible adds an exclamation mark:

Sh'ma, Yisra'el! ADONAI Eloheinu, ADONAI echad
[Hear, Isra'el! ADONAI our God, ADONAI is one].[11]

Keep in mind, Deuteronomy 6:4 is technically considered the Shema all by itself. In an ancient world burgeoning with religious and cultic practices, prayers, and sacrifices offered to innumerable gods, YHWH intended Israel to understand that he was an absolute stand-alone. *Listen, Israel: The LORD our God, the LORD is one.*

Before another word was said, they were to hear, absorb, and reaffirm the irrevocable, immutable oneness and separateness of God. YHWH used no uncertain terms to convey that to add any other so-called god to him was to automatically subtract him from the equation. The only answer to the question they'd sung after crossing the Red Sea, "LORD, who is like you among the gods?" (Exodus 15:11) was unequivocally "No one!"

Dr. Ellen F. Davis is among the foremost scholars of the Old Testament Scriptures. We'll look to her expertise in the following excerpt from her book *Opening Israel's Scriptures*:

> God's oneness is not an impersonal numerical formulation. Rather, it is the fundamental biblical statement about God's nature, which is complete and self-consistent. God's oneness calls forth Israel's own oneness—its single-heartedness toward God. Thus, God's nature is the basis for the reciprocal commitment that is covenant.[12]

Complete this sentence from Dr. Davis's excerpt: God's oneness calls forth

__________ ______ ____________________________ — its __________________ -

______________________________ toward God.

That's Deuteronomy's covenant in a nutshell. In essence God is saying, "I have chosen you. Your part, if you obey, is to choose me, but you must know that to choose me is to choose only me and to do so with all that is in you. I have also set my perfect affections upon you. Your part, if you obey, is to set your whole affections (though imperfect and insufficient) on me."

Some aspects of covenant terminology in Deuteronomy echo ancient Assyrian treaties between lords and vassals, but the Lord's relational involvement extends well beyond typical ancient treaties. His involvement with the Israelites was no mere arrangement. He professed his affection for them over and over. He called them his treasured possession and spoke of how he'd brought them to himself on eagles' wings (Exodus 19:4-6).

How thoroughly did God call upon his people to love him, according to Deuteronomy 6:5?

From the start, love for God was devotion put into action. Not only was it enacted in worship of God, but God himself considered that worship inconsequential and basically irrelevant if it did not move his people into godly interaction with others. You and I study these verses from the vantage point of the complete canon comprising the Christian Bible. From this side of history, we have more context for God's commands in the scope of his entire inspired Word. God alone can give what God requires. It takes God to serve God. Everything we have to give to God in reciprocal love and devotion must be drawn from the well of what we have first received from God.

- "We love because [God] first loved us" (1 John 4:19).
- "Dear friends, let us love one another, because love is from God" (1 John 4:7).

In this same vein, fill in the following blanks according to 1 John 4:16:

We have ________________________________

and ______________________________ the

__________________ that God has for us.

Romans 5:5 describes the wonder that enables us to love beyond our human capacity:

God's love has been poured out in our hearts
through the Holy Spirit who was given to us.

Finally, let's look at Deuteronomy 6:6-9.

These words that I am giving you today are to be in your heart. Repeat them to your children. Talk about them when you sit in your house and when you walk along the road, when you lie down and when you get up. Bind them as a sign on your hand and let them be a symbol on your forehead. Write them on the doorposts of your house and on your city gates.

These commands came to be practiced in myriad ways in Judaism, on a graduating spectrum from the strictly metaphorical to the most literal. For example, even today in the Old City of Jerusalem, you might walk past Orthodox Jewish men with small boxes on their foreheads, arms or hands affixed with bands as a sign of their devotion to God (Deuteronomy 6:8). Inside the boxes are verses from the Torah (often Exodus 13:1-10; Deuteronomy 6:4-9; 11:13-21) in smallest imaginable print. A mezuzah may be more familiar to us on this side of the world. It's a small metal container affixed to the doorpost that houses miniature pages with a tiny printing of Deuteronomy 6:4-9 and 11:13-21.

While we're right to respect these Orthodox practices, even more important is the motive behind them. Many would argue that the heart of the law is the point of the passages. *These words that I am giving you today are to be in your heart.* In other words, from the heart utterly attached to God flows the fully integrated life with God. This idea should sound familiar to us by now because it is reminiscent of the ideas communicated by Brother Lawrence as he practiced God's presence and Eugene Peterson as he studied the Old Testament in "conscious company with Jesus."

Our aim in this study is to learn how to walk more closely with God based on what we learn about those who walked with God in five chronological eras of history. So after setting the original text within its cultural context, we are well within our aim to ask how these examples might lend insight into our walk with God today. How do we teach this God-life to our children? Our grandchildren? Our nieces and nephews? The children in our churches?

Each generation is called to parent the next in the things of God. **In what ways have you been parented well in the walk of faith? What approaches have you used when passing on faith to the next generation? Which of these approaches seemed to work best?**

As an addendum, I'll share a little about my own wobbly attempts to integrate the teachings in Deuteronomy 6:6-9 into my parenting, in case any part of it might be beneficial.

You don't get through long-term parenting unscathed. Neither do your children. That's simply a fact of life for unfinished humans on this side of the veil. The goal is to help them as much as possible and harm them as little as possible. I have many regrets. We certainly did not have the perfect home or, at times, even a stable home. We were by no stretch of the imagination a poster Christian family. Keith and I not only had our own sinful, selfish natures, we brought scars and wounds from our families of origin into our marriage, and they were not without effect on each other or on our children.

Despite some very hard and unhappy circumstances, I somehow managed to derive a significant amount of joy in Christ. I do mean stubborn joy. Joy that could be suppressed but never for long. This, of course, was not of my own doing, and apart from grace, I have no comprehension why it was God's doing. But it was the God of this stubborn joy, this God who was ever redeeming my past, this God of inexplicable rescue and cleansing of sins at the cost of his own life, this God so beautifully, powerfully, and tenderly shown us in the Scriptures that I most wanted to teach to my children. I deeply wanted my daughters to know right from wrong and how God's ways differed from the ways of this world, but even more, I wanted them to trust his motives. I wanted them to know that his commands were driven by divine unconditional love and were always for our good and our flourishing.

To the degree that any of my efforts worked, they overflowed from what God was doing in my own heart. Yes, we who parent, stepparent, or spiritually parent could practice a Deuteronomy 6:7 kind of approach by rule, rote, and sheer intention. *Repeat them to your children. Talk about them when you sit in your house and when you walk along the road, when you lie down and when you get up.* We could say, do, and teach all the right things apart from our own hearts and souls being nourished by intimacy with God, but those we teach would eventually catch on to that.

Children are perceptive—and more so than we wish at times. They recognize hypocrisies in their growing-up years no matter how well we try to hide them. They can feel what is real. Don't misunderstand me to say that we only teach God's ways when we feel like it. Jesus insists in Luke 6:45, however, that the mouth speaks out of the overflow of the heart. This truth indicates that the best way to integrate Jesus into our everyday conversations at home and in all the coming and going with our children is to constantly let him teach and tend to and pour his love into our own hearts. Then the rest comes organically.

My daughters are grown-ups now, with their own busy lives. I talked with both of them before I wrote this part of the lesson. You see, you don't get to be my age without having seen and endured enough to scar you and rid you of a certain amount of sentimentality and convenient naivete. They were raised by a mother fully immersed in Christian culture.

They've seen leaders fall. They've seen hypocrisy. They've seen human doctrines disguised as doctrines of God. They've seen the Scriptures exploited for human power. They've seen the dark side of legalism and hyper-fundamentalism, of purity culture rampant during their adolescence, of gender bias, of women's silence and subjugation sold as biblical submission. They have each nearly bled out at times from church hurt. All the while, they have by no means been oblivious to weaknesses of character and lapses of integrity in their own mother. So I had questions for each of them before I spoke into this topic, lest they read this someday with disdain.

"Did you resent it?" I asked them separately on the same day. "Did you resent how you were raised? You know, how much we talked about Jesus and all. Went to church and did all the things?"

I knew they'd answer me honestly, because that's their way. Our way as a family. They drew some distinctions between church and home, saying, yes, they sometimes resented church.

"But, no, Mom," each of them said separately, "I didn't resent the way you taught and talked about Jesus." In a modern twist of talking God-things while "walking along the road," both spoke with great affection and laughter of the copious coming and going we did in the car, singing praise songs and contemporary Christian music at the top of our lungs. "Those are good memories. Some of the best memories," one said. They didn't claim to resent the many Jesus-oriented conversations and prayers over math tests, friend drama, basketball and volleyball games.

They let go of a lot of things. But Jesus held.

By grace alone, Jesus held. Though institutions fell from their pedestals and people didn't come through and some religious practices and high-hype styles of preaching, praying, and worshiping would sour on them, Jesus held.

It didn't have to go that way. Kids have been raised to love Jesus by far better and more genuine parents and still chosen to leave the Christian faith. There is no sure formula. God said of his own children in the eleventh chapter of Hosea,

When Israel was a child, I loved him,
and out of Egypt I called my son. . . .
It was I who taught Ephraim to walk,
taking them by the hand,
but they never knew that I healed them.
I led them with human cords,
with ropes of love.

HOSEA 11:1, 3-4

And yet he said,

> My people are bent on turning from me.
>
> HOSEA 11:7

But here is what I know: What anchors us behind the veil is Jesus. Religious ways cannot save us. Good choices and moral lives can do us many favors, but they cannot earn us abundant life. Waiting until our wedding day to have sex doesn't guarantee a happy or successful marriage. Tithing won't guarantee you can pay your house note. Raising kids in church does not ensure they'll stay in church. Naming-and-claiming doesn't work. The prosperity gospel will prove a very expensive farce. But teaching and conveying with the lived-out life that Jesus is Lord—that Jesus is life, that Jesus is light and in him is no darkness, that the cross is big enough to cleanse us from every sin, that one sweet day for all who believe in him there will be no more night, and that all pain and sorrow and death will pass away—will indeed mean one thing: You haven't lied. You told the truth. And his name is Jesus.

Delights

Perplexities

Sighings

RECORDKEEPER FOR YOUR WALK

Laments

Word Alerts

Divine Consolations/Comforts

Perceived Presence

WEEK 3

the HEART *of* WALKING

SESSION 3

The Heart of Walking

You can fill in these blanks as you watch the video for session 3.

Introduction: Our goal in our present study is to glean insight into our own walks with God by viewing what walking with God looked like in five chronological eras of biblical history. We launched with *the genesis*, or "The Beginning of Walking," then followed it with "The Law of Walking," and now we move forward to "The ______________________________."

A Quick Overview of the Psalter

Book 1: Chapters ________ (predominantly Davidic psalms)

Book 2: Chapters ________ (psalms of Korah and Asaph unfold)

Book 3: Chapters ________ (nearly exclusively psalms of Korah and Asaph)

Book 4: Chapters ________ (predominantly untitled psalms)

Book 5: Chapters ________ (contains multiple pilgrimage songs to Temple and feasts)

Of the psalms ascribed to certain writers, David wrote approximately _______.
Asaph: ___ / Sons of Korah: ___ / Solomon: ___ / Moses, Heman, and Ethan each wrote _____.

Around ____ psalms are anonymous.

Consider these points:

1. Walking with God does not mean incessantly _____________ with God. Walking with God is more like moving with him through the variegated seasons and ______________ emotions of life in a __________________ with _____________.

2. The ___________________ of the human to the divine in this shared space is generally called ______________.

3. No form of prayer has more capacity to _____________ and ___________ the human than song.

In the book *Opening Israel's Scriptures*, Old Testament theologian Ellen Davis writes,

> The practical value of psalms is that they encourage those who read them to bring to the work of theology the ____________ of __________ capacity and _______________, to integrate those several domains that modern culture often insists on _______________________. Reading psalms well requires the effort of deep engagement, since good poetry cannot be read in a distracted or detached state.[1]

Consider a cross section of psalms for taking the pulse on the heart of walking.

Read Psalm 51:6-13. Note verse 7: "The prayer is literally to be '_______________________ with ____________________.'"[2]

Video session available for purchase at ***TyndaleChristianResources.com****.*

A young college professor by the name of John Ronald Reuel Tolkien had his head down grading exams one day when he paused a second, tugged on a piece of scrap paper, and jotted down a single sentence. "In a hole in the ground there lived a hobbit." The sentence sat by itself for a good many years, with nothing added to it or taken away. Any parent knows that a house full of children can drive respectable adults to their wits' end. Tolkien's, on the other hand, drove him to his pen. From that solitary sentence would burgeon an elaborate tale told in prose, poetry, riddles, and songs written for the amusement of his own children.

Early in the gargantuan story, Tolkien's protagonist, Bilbo Baggins, is dazzled by a song of doom and dragons sung by dwarves, ending with these words:

Far over the misty mountains grim
To dungeons deep and caverns dim
We must away, ere break of day,
To win our harps and gold from him!

Tolkien writes of the protagonist,

> Then something Tookish woke up inside him, and he wished to go and see the great mountains, and hear the pine-trees and the waterfalls, and explore the caves, and wear a sword instead of a walking-stick. He looked out of the window. The stars were out in a dark sky above the trees. He thought of the jewels of the dwarves shining in dark caverns. Suddenly in the wood beyond The Water a flame leapt up—probably somebody lighting a wood-fire—and he thought of plundering dragons settling on his quiet Hill and kindling it all to flames. He shuddered; and very quickly he was plain Mr. Baggins of Bag-End, Under-Hill, again. He got up trembling. He had less than half a mind to fetch the lamp, and more than half a mind to pretend to, and go and hide behind the beer-barrels in the cellar.[3]

This is what I'm praying for you this week: that something Tookish wakes up in you. Something adventurous and daring. Something that can never easily go back to sleep. Like us real folks, fictional Bilbo came from two family lines: his father's (the Bagginses) and his mother's (the Tooks). The Bagginses were the careful sort. Proper. Annoyed by interruptions and troubled by risk. The Tooks, in their estimation, were silly sorts, wasting proper thoughts on wild imaginings. Going about when they should have been staying in. Perhaps Bilbo's arteries were too stiff and thin for his Took blood. He was Baggins to the bone till one fateful day, when an old man with a long gray beard and a blue pointy hat showed up on his doorstep and helped himself into his home. Gandalf, the visitor, made haste to state his intentions.

> I am looking for someone to share in an adventure that I am arranging, and it's very difficult to find anyone.[4]

Baggins replied,

> I should think so—in these parts! We are plain quiet folk and have no use for adventures. Nasty disturbing uncomfortable things! Make you late for dinner![5]

Soon, of course, came the song, and "something Tookish woke up inside him." It can happen to the most devoted Bagginses among us. A song can wake us up to a world far more daring than we imagined. Not less true, but more so. Not less honest, but more honest.

That's certainly the case in my interview with Malcolm Guite. If you aren't familiar with him, I can't wait to introduce you.* He's unforgettable. I love the balance he strikes in his marvelous book, *The Word Within the Words*:

> How then should we read scripture? There is a place for study, for scholarship, for exposition, but the deepest way is meditation, is contemplating and reciting these scriptures in the presence of and in conversation with Christ. As Saint Paul says: "let the word of Christ dwell in you richly." We need both the words, and the Word. We need the Word undergirding the words, the Word shimmering through the words. This is how I have approached the scriptures both as a believer and a poet.[6]

*  *Find Beth's interview with Malcolm Guite here.*

NOTES

DAY 1

With you I can attack a barricade, and with my God I can leap over a wall.

PSALM 18:29

All that is gold does not glitter, not all those who wander are lost.

GANDALF, *THE LORD OF THE RINGS*

We're entering the genre of biblical poetry this week through the lens of the psalter's era to search out "The Heart of Walking." This excerpt from *The Hobbit* may seem a strange welcome to the week, until we recount how the rhythmic winds of adventure and song blew open his airtight imagination. Our path takes us not to Middle Earth but to the middle of our Bibles and a bit beyond, where we find psalms and songs of ecstasy, victory, doom, threat, promises, judgment, love, grace, and despair.

We find cosmic battles with arrows flying and hear the voice like thunder that shatters cedars. You see, imagination is not synonymous with fiction. Fiction requires the imagination, but not all that is imagined is fiction. And not all that is nonfiction is literal. **Can you think of an example of the intersection of imagination and reality, whether within the Bible or outside of it? If so, share it here.**

Over and again on the pages of Scripture, God is out to capture the imaginations of his people—spokesmen and spokeswomen, listeners and readers alike—with figurative language, figures of speech, metaphors, parables, hyperbole, parallelism, similes, and so forth to illustrate a point of truth or to memorably convey a message. We see these features in numerous psalms. Under the inspiration of the Holy Spirit, David seeks refuge in the shadow of God's wings (Psalm 57:1), but we're not left to think God is a hen. In the same psalm, the songwriter also describes being "surrounded by lions" and lying down "among devouring lions." Few can claim such an experience until the psalmist does us the favor of interpreting the word picture: "People whose teeth are spears and arrows, whose tongues are sharp swords" (Psalm 57:4). Suddenly, few of us can claim not to have experienced this.

In a crude nutshell, most imaginations are impoverished when it comes to God. One of our tasks this week is to invite God to feed our impoverished imaginations with Scripture. Psalm 18:1-19 is a grand place to begin. Read this section of Scripture aloud like you're reading it to a class of college students you want to hear it and feel it in a way the psalm deserves. Read it as if you yourself wrote it. Ride the ups and downs of it, changing your pace, rhythm, and volume according to how you imagine David reciting it.

Psalm 18 is exquisite biblical poetry, isn't it? Through these verses the Holy Spirit overtakes the pen of David to reveal the man as poet, yes, but, higher still, God, the inspirer, as poet. Taken even further, we see the inspirer as painter. Every stroke of the brush creates a scene intended to sweep its reader and hearer into it. God paints pictures with words to convey what statements of facts cannot.

Note the metaphors David uses for God in Psalm 18:2. What does that two-letter word you find before several of them tell you about God? ("_____ rock . . .")

I'd love to have heard you read the dramatic theophany in verses 7-15. In his commentary on Psalm 18, scholar Gerald H. Wilson makes sure we don't gloss over the scene as if it's "business as usual."

> The narrative of deliverance now moves to an extended theophany, in which the approach of God into the profane world of human existence is described with all its fearsome effects. The awesome power and majesty of the divine glory entering the

> human world is not business as usual. God's holy otherness places sinful humanity under threat, and even the created order suffers by direct exposure to his presence. The created world cannot contain the creator, and its usual laws and order are stretched to the breaking point by this divine intrusion.[7]

Absorb how in this imagery God stirs up the storm then uses it to ride where he desires to go. When we are in a storm, he'll use the very winds threatening us to blow in to save us. Consider the divine being doing all this for one solitary human. We might imagine the Lord going to such extravagance for a king like David or a strategic leader in any generation, since rescuing the one would be tantamount to rescuing many. Jesus, however, begs to differ in Luke 15:3-7, as the shepherd who leaves the ninety-nine for the one lost sheep and, upon finding it, calls his neighbors over to rejoice with him.

Scholar Derek Kidner affirms God's generosity in this respect:

> The titanic scale of this scene is in strange contrast to the small human figure of the singer, to rescue whom God does battle in person against *death* and *perdition* (4, 5), armed with his most fearsome weapons. Such is the worth, the psalm implies, of an individual, and such is that individual's debt to God. King though David is, the whole psalm is in the singular and has the freshness of personal experience. David is blessed because God has "delighted" (19) in him, not simply because he represents his people.[8]

These considerations stir up a question profoundly relevant to our walking with God. **Do you see yourself—all by yourself—as worth God's dramatic effort? Expound on your truthful answer, whether yes or no.**

Now move to Psalm 18:16:

He reached down from on high
and took hold of me;
he pulled me out of deep water.

Reflect on the last time you felt you were in deep water. Sometimes a singular thing is pulling us under the water like a thick rope on our ankle connected to a seventy-pound anvil. Other times, an accumulation of concerns and demands threatens to drown us, as if we're attached to multiple ropes, each dangling with ten-pound weights. **Which is most reflective of the last time you felt like you were drowning in your circumstances? Offer a brief description.**

The next verse reads with reprieve:

> He rescued me from my powerful enemy
> and from those who hated me,
> for they were too strong for me.

I well recall coming to grips with the reality of having a very real enemy who completely outpowered me with troops that far outnumbered my most prayerful comrades and me. Camp on the word *hated*. **Have you ever felt hated? If so, by whom?**

In retrospect, did your sense of being hated turn out to be accurate, or did time prove it to be skewed? Explain.

Hatred can feel like a superpower. It can make a mere human feel inordinately strong. Dislike harbors negativity, but hatred wishes harm. With its obsessive hold on the mind, hate can't think straight. These observations might shed light on how the apostle John could compare hatred with murder (1 John 3:15). I've nurtured varying degrees of dislike toward numerous people along the way, but I felt what I considered authentic hatred toward two. The feeling was terrifying and ultimately miserable enough to goad me into seeking deliverance before many months passed. At least for me, hatred was the furthest thing from not caring. Oh, I cared all right. I cared that the person would be as miserable as I was.

I'd formerly loved the individuals I then hated, a fact beyond coincidence. A fine line can exist between love and hate, can't it? Perhaps the depth to which we've loved and trusted a person is the depth to which we can, under bad enough conditions, hate and feel betrayed by a person. Maybe the vacuum left by the loss of love begs to be filled and, apart from God, all we have to give it is hate. I'm no psychologist. These have simply been my experiences. At the end of the season, the way I'd shifted to hate to help anesthetize the hurt became remarkably clear. I'd done it simply because hate made me feel powerful. Hurt just *hurt*, making me feel weak and pathetic. What I had to learn in that treacherous stretch is that God doesn't promise to empower the powerful. He promises to strengthen the weak. The hate I'd turned to in order to protect my heart had only postponed my healing.

Tell me I'm not alone. **What has been your experience with hatred?**

Let these thoughts accrue as you proceed to Psalm 18:18:

They confronted me in the day of my calamity,
but the LORD was my support.

Satan fights dirty, as do those willing to do his bidding. He takes advantage of your worst moments, losses, tragedies, and crises when he can. He will happily kick you when you're down, then shame you for not getting up. Satan can hit us at any point—and certainly our high points—to block the joy we were meant to find in them. Our present task, however, is to enter David's experience in the eighteenth psalm. Here he speaks of being confronted in a time of calamity or, in the NIV wording, "the day of my disaster." **Has the enemy ever come for you at a time that was already calamitous or disastrous enough? If so, describe how you feel he took advantage of it.**

"But the LORD was my support." Sometimes we won't know the Lord has been supporting us all along until we're on the other side of the hateful season. **Are you able to see in retrospect how the Lord supported you? Honesty is crucial to our walk with God, so please don't think you need to say yes.**

Just two more verses and we'll close. Psalm 18:19 reads,

He brought me out to a spacious place;
he rescued me because he delighted in me.

Are you genuinely able to process the fact that God delights in you? That he came to your rescue not out of mere obligation? Or out of baseline toleration?

One way to get insight into your authentic take on divine rescue is whether you feel like you were brought to a spacious place or you were put on probation. **What has been the case for you? Explain your answer.**

So much changes in your walk with God when you come to believe the rock-solid truth that the Savior of the world delights in *you*. We are finally freed to delight in Jesus when we can embrace in our most hidden places that he delights in us. And this, fellow sojourner, brings us to our final point. We'll find it back at the beginning. **What is the very first thing David says to God in Psalm 18?**

"______________________________, Lord . . ."

There you have it: the characteristic above all others that made David a man after God's own heart. He took the love God had for him as not only security but capacity and loved him right back with it. He had come to believe he belonged to God, and therefore God belonged to him. In this reciprocal possessiveness ignited by rescue, real love was born.

DAY 2

Hear my prayer, LORD . . .

PSALM 39:12

Intimidation is as fatal to prayer as distraction.

EUGENE H. PETERSON, *ANSWERING GOD*

Today's entry is between the Lord and you, with no interference from me once I offer instructions. Your assignment is to handwrite the segments of Scripture you'll find in the left-hand margin. The idea is to write these verses in the exact order given, without any break between them. Completed, the writing should look like one composition. Since you already have the references, please don't include them in the writing so the flow is uninterrupted. After you've handwritten all the verses, go back to the beginning and pray aloud the whole prayer, as if it is coming from your own lips. My hope is that you'll find it meaningful enough to return to it and read it in the days to come.

If we had all five weeks to study only the psalter, we could read a marvelous number of David's psalms from the first to last verse, asking God to make the singer's passion contagious. Our aim in this study, however, narrows the focus considerably. We're taking this one week to mine treasures of the psalter to demonstrate the vital connection between our heart toward God and our walk with God. Days 1, 2, and 3 of our current week each direct us to segments in psalms written either by or for David, since God called him a man after his own heart.

Here are a few notes before you begin.

All of the verses I've selected are prayers of David addressed directly to God rather than to the congregation *about* God. The psalms offer innumerable benefits. Their importance to the canon is inestimable. Nothing is more significant to us in this study, however, than this: The psalms are teachers of prayer, tutoring the walk of the willing disciple, transforming their life.

The aim is to record the Scriptures precisely, but by all means, use any Bible translation you like. If copying the exact words is too constraining for you, far better to freestyle with your own words than forgo the assignment, so be free! Just make sure you mirror the meaning.

Okay, then. I'll leave it to you and the Lord from here.

PSALM 61:1-3

PSALM 9:1-2

PSALM 5:4

PSALM 63:3

PSALM 5:1-2

PSALM 38:9

PSALM 39:7-8

PSALM 6:2

PSALM 3:3

PSALM 17:8

PSALM 31:16

PSALM 31:19

PSALM 9:10

PSALM 10:17-18

PSALM 3:8

PSALM 16:5

PSALM 16:11

PSALM 65:4

PSALM 30:11-12

PSALM 18:1

DAY 3

This poor man cried . . .

PSALM 34:6

The last temptation is the greatest treason: / To do the right deed for the wrong reason.

T. S. ELIOT, *MURDER IN THE CATHEDRAL*

We still have fascinating places to go with the psalter on days 4 and 5 in our search for "The Heart of Walking," but this is our final segment to spend exclusively with David. Let's soak it in. We've taken extra time on psalms written by or for David since God set him in an exceptional category by calling him a man after his own heart (1 Samuel 13:14). What's more impressive is how God did not bother expunging the reference when David was old and on his deathbed, world weary and sin scarred. The sacred songbook has reams of pages reflecting the relational dynamics between God and David. We will end our time in David's writings by peering into a dynamic of inestimable impact on any walk with God.

Your challenge today is to closely investigate Psalm 32 and Psalm 51 for every possible indication or innuendo regarding David's view of two elements:

- the gravity of sin
- the forgiveness of sin

Record what you find in the spaces that follow, jotting down the verse references that suggest or support each element you list.

PSALM 32

The gravity of sin	The forgiveness of sin

PSALM 51

The gravity of sin	The forgiveness of sin

What appears to be the role of confession in these two psalms, according to David?

Do you think confession is necessary? Why or why not? List all the reasons that come to mind.

You and I have the privilege of living this side of the cross and resurrection of Jesus Christ. We're told that "while we were yet sinners, Christ died for us" (Romans 5:8, KJV). We were still "dead in trespasses and in the uncircumcision of [our] flesh" when God made us alive with Christ and "forgave us all our trespasses" (Colossians 2:13). According to Colossians 2:14, God "erased the certificate of debt, with its obligations, that was against us and opposed to us," taking it away "by nailing it to the cross." If, in relying entirely on Christ for salvation, the payment for all our sins has already been made in full, why would we need to confess our sin? **Use the margins on each side of 1 John 1:6-10 to note any reasons offered, then draw a line connecting each to the supporting verse or phrase.**

If we say, "We have fellowship with
him," and yet we walk in darkness,
we are lying and are not practicing
the truth. If we walk in the light as
he himself is in the light, we have
fellowship with one another, and the
blood of Jesus his Son cleanses us
from all sin. If we say, "We have no
sin," we are deceiving ourselves, and
the truth is not in us. If we confess
our sins, he is faithful and righteous
to forgive us our sins and to cleanse
us from all unrighteousness. If we
say, "We have not sinned," we make
him a liar, and his word is not in us.

1 JOHN 1:6-10

We could end all discussion with the simple truth that we confess our sins because God tells us to and we're called to obedience intended for our good, not our harm. But God didn't end the discussion there. Instead, we're promised unrestrained forgiveness and complete cleansing. What a relief to those who dare to believe!

God knows us infinitely better than we know ourselves. Sometimes our own mouths have to do the speaking for our own ears to do the hearing. We cannot repent of what we will not own, and we will seldom own what we will not speak.

Sometimes our own mouths have to do the speaking for our own ears to do the hearing.

First John 1:6-10 communicates the fruit of confession with profound relevance to our theme. Confessing sin and receiving divine cleansing maintains fellowship with God in our walk with him.

The Greek word for confess is "ὁμολογέω *homologéō*; . . . which is from *homoú*, together with, and *légō*, to say."[9] It means to say in agreement with something already said. God says, for example, that coveting is wrong, so when I covet and confess it, I'm saying in effect, "Lord, I agree with you that coveting what belongs to someone else is wrong and that, in doing so, I've sinned."

Sin disrupts fellowship. Agreeing that it does to the point of repentance restores fellowship.

The distance unconfessed sin creates in our walk with the Lord is not so much in proximity. God is omnipresent, always near. The distance creeps into our communion with God. Remember, good behavior is not what God is after most in his relationship with us. It's engagement. Fellowship. What God desires most is that we most desire God and that we desire least what comes between us.

Take care not to confuse disruption with silence. God is merciful and often still communicates with us long after we'd deserve an impenetrable ceiling. As for us, we never talk faster to the Lord than when we're trying to keep from hearing the Holy Spirit bring up that sin. We can go days on end praying like nothing is amiss, but we've stopped talking *honestly*. When we realize our intimacy with God is suffering and respond to the conviction of the Holy Spirit, confession is the way we return to honest conversation, and honest conversation is the way we're restored to fellowship.

Take a good look at the evidences you recorded from each psalm regarding David's take on the gravity and forgiveness of sin, glancing back over the psalms for reminders of connections.

Behold David's astonishing understanding of God. Were these two elements the sum of his comprehension, we'd still have reason to be impressed. He managed to hold tightly to two truths at once that, in my observation, we're often tempted (if not taught) to choose between.

Have you ever been in a Christian environment that took sin much more seriously than forgiveness? Or forgiveness much more seriously than sin? Describe it here:

If you're in a community of faith that takes both sin and the forgiveness of sin seriously, bless the Lord, who has led you well. Consider what can happen when either one is expendable. Pounding relentlessly on the dreadfulness of sin while whispering about the outpouring of grace through forgiveness not only misrepresents God, it can produce the rotting fruit of hopelessness, despair, authoritarianism, secrecy, or rigid legalism, quenching the Spirit and elevating confidence in the flesh. **What comes to your mind that I overlooked?**

On the other hand, triumphant celebration of the marvels of grace and forgiveness with little grasp of the gravity of sin also misrepresents God. The fruit of this disproportion is also poisonous. It can stunt growth in Christ, undermine sanctification, impair conviction, excuse wrongdoing, upend repentance, and mass-produce people who won't take responsibility for their actions. **Anything else you want to add?**

Each without the other tragically diminishes our view of the power of the cross, blurring the beauty of forgiveness. If I lack an adequate understanding of both sin and forgiveness, how can I ever fully appreciate and act on my freedom in Christ? I believe each imbalance also cultivates an environment where abuse can thrive. **If you agree, why do you think this is true? If you don't agree, explain why you see it differently.**

David was well versed in the perilousness of sin, both in its intrinsic wrong (as antithetical to God's holiness and goodness) and its reverberating consequences. He'd been wronged by many and wronged many, and haven't we all? "For we all stumble in many ways," James 3:2 reads, and that includes David. An overview of his songs indicates, however, that David was miserable enough in his sins to seek a fast exit. In an authentic walk with God, the places we wander outside his will grow increasingly inhospitable. Anyone can fall into sin (Galatians 6:1), but if our consciences haven't been seared against the work of the Holy Spirit, we grow increasingly unhappy there.

What makes David such a cautionary tale is the height from which he fell. He was a true worshiper, a lover of Torah, a tenacious and victorious warrior, God's anointed one, wearing the crown of an everlasting kingdom. He had it all. Then somewhere along the way, David took those riches God had graced upon him and bought his own press. Increasingly bored by what belonged to him, he demanded what did not.

He saw a woman he wanted and "sent messengers to get her" (2 Samuel 11:4). When he had satiated himself, David sent her back and washed his hands of her. Then she turned up pregnant. What's a king to do? This one summoned her husband from the battlefield, assuming he'd go home and have sex with his wife, then later assume the baby was his. David underestimated Uriah's integrity, however. Uriah would give himself no such luxury, since his fellow soldiers were still camped in the open field.

So David had him killed. Let that sink in. He likely thought he'd gotten away with it until God told what he'd done to a prophet named Nathan, who confronted David with his sins, cutting his calloused conscience to the quick, bringing him to his knees. Psalm 51 was written in the wake of David's repentance from this season of rupturing sin.

This, my friend, is why David's firm grasp on both the gravity of sin and the forgiveness of sin is particularly moving. Fast-forward to the New Testament, where you find Saul turned Paul, a captor and murderer of Jesus-followers who was called by God, forgiven all his sins, and used as powerfully as any one saint in Scripture (see Acts 9). Neither ever got over the grace of God. They are far from the only ones.

I don't know many people personally who've been more tormented by chronic regret than I. I'm talking about the kind that makes a person sick and cruelly snatches happy moments before they can sink in. The kind that confuses consequences with God's unremitting displeasure. What makes this chronic regret worth mentioning here is the staggering number of years it lasted after I'd repented from those grievous sins and foolish choices and not turned back. The more I came to love Jesus, the worthier of faithfulness I saw him and the more I regretted my foolishness. At my lowest moments, I felt so crushed by remorse, I wished God would shorten my life just for the sake of relief. "I can't bear the weight of this, Lord." He alone knows how many times I said those words to him before this truth got loud enough in my heart for me to finally hear.

We can't both bear the weight of your sins, Beth.

Even knowing it to be true wasn't an instant fix. Gradually the old voice of condemnation faded into songs of deliverance tuned to the heartstrings of God's unquenchable love. In time I came to see my insistence on shouldering the burden of my forgiven sins as an insult to the cross of Christ: His death apparently wasn't enough for me. I needed to supplement it with my misery.

Who was I to see myself and my sins as bigger than David and his? Paul and his? Every other faltering person in the canon of Scripture and theirs? God's grace was enough for them but not enough for me? Does that sound a tad arrogant to you?

I wonder if any part of my experience strikes a chord with you or reminds you of someone you love. If so, explain how.

If living the rest of our lives with chronic regret and relentless self-condemnation over sin that God has forgiven and we've walked away from isn't what honors Christ, what does? Well, humility for one, seeing no sin as beyond us. And no sin as beyond the cross. Two, a deeper commitment to holiness. And three? **I'll let David answer that one for you from his own pen in Psalm 32:1-2.**

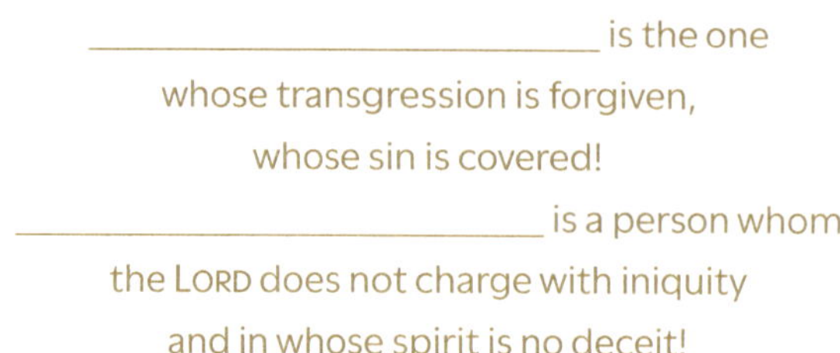

________________________ is the one
whose transgression is forgiven,
whose sin is covered!
________________________ is a person whom
the LORD does not charge with iniquity
and in whose spirit is no deceit!

Imagine that. Being happy about forgiveness! I say we give it a shot.

These verses provide a perfect ending. You're welcome to conclude right here. This has been a long lesson, no doubt in part because the subject matter has been a long road for me personally. If you want to hang around another minute, I'll tell you a story from the early years of my marriage. You need not be married to get the point.

Keith and I stood at the altar straight out of college, having clearly negotiated a package deal. I was to accept his hunting and fishing, and he was to accept my neck-deep immersion in all things church. We moved a few times in our first several years and had two babies, but by the time they were little more than toddlers, we were settled in a large church in Houston, where we'd remain some twenty-seven years. By the first time we walked through those church doors, Keith should've had ample opportunity to learn the fine art of faking it, but alas, he chose this of all occasions to be a slow learner.

Apparently overcome by conviction one morning, he confided to his all-men's Sunday school class that he struggled with lust. One of the men then confided to his wife that Keith struggled with lust. His wife then confided to me that Keith struggled with lust, and soon after, no doubt to strengthen our prayer covering, obviously confided to others in our all-women's Sunday school class that Keith struggled with lust. By the time we entered Sunday school the next week, everyone looked at us with palpable pity that Keith—you guessed it—struggled with lust.

And I, his wife, was clearly not enough for him.

Perhaps I need not say we hardly made it through the front door of our home before I sent our little girls out to play and commenced to confide to Keith how I felt about him confiding with his all-men's Sunday school class that he struggled with lust.

He hung his head and said, "I thought I could."

I was furious for days and wounded for months. I was too young and knew too little about life not to take his admission deeply personally. This much I could reason: We deserved it, anyway. *Didn't we?* After all, we were the most messed-up couple in our large Sunday school department, even without Keith's confessions. We'd earned our shame. Earned our place as the couple least likely to succeed. We might as well own it.

Years passed. Decades passed. And time has a way of telling secrets. I'm not glad about that. It's just a fact. Several active couples in our all-marrieds Sunday school department split up, and a few others aged enough to begin sharing their turbulent stories. Other couples maintained the stance of those above reproach, and I really don't even doubt their authenticity. Well, maybe I doubt a few. I'm still a work in progress.

I share this story with you not out of spite or vindication. I didn't relish the news of the troubles of other couples even when they surfaced. Life's hard. Marriage is hard. Even though I imagine many of the men and women in our classes battled wrong desires, I don't share this story thinking others should've admitted it. But I do wish Keith had been right when he said, "I thought I could." He shouldn't have had to hang his head. He should've been able to share it. Anyone should've. A good place and a safe space can be two very different things.

I share the story for one solitary reason: that you who are a long way from perfect in an environment that appears frighteningly close to it might not feel alone. We did. And I don't want you to. Because the fact is, you're not. I don't care how silent people may become when you share what you're going through in hopes of feeling less shamed and more reassured. Nobody out there has life figured out. Nobody knows until he or she has been there what it's like to feel avalanched by trials or temptations, personal or spiritual attacks, family calamities, intolerable loneliness, mental anguish, chronic pain, betrayal, depression, rejection, loss, or anything else and be either too poorly equipped, caught off guard, or weak willed to deal successfully with it.

Not all fall into defeat under these kinds of conditions, but all, I believe, who are awake enough before the Lord to be paying attention are humbled by a bombarding season of temptation, knowing only by the grace of God and the skin of their teeth did they escape those flames without getting scorched.

DAY 4

When the king asked the woman, she told him the story.

2 KINGS 8:6

Every day is a story, a morning beginning and evening ending that are boundaries for people who go about their tasks with more or less purpose, go to war, make love, earn a living, scheme and sin and believe. Everything is connected. Meaning is everywhere. The days add up to a life that is a story.

EUGENE H. PETERSON, *ANSWERING GOD*

I think you should write. I think you should find out what kind of ink God has stored in the well of your soul. That is, if you haven't already dipped a pen into it. I'm not talking about writing to publish. If God has you on that trajectory, I'd be immensely pleased for him to use something in this lesson to encourage you. If you're an established author, I'd be honored to cheer you on. But the kind of writing I long to recommend doesn't require shopping a manuscript or building a social media following.

I'm talking about discovering, nurturing, and developing, under divine tutelage, your own way of written expression that surfaces only where it's safest and births a satisfaction that can't be bought. Those to whom writing comes most easily can be the least likely to find their truest God-given voices because they don't have to work that hard. Why plunge the deep when enough treasures float? Nothing's wrong with drawing from what's most accessible. But wouldn't it be a shame if you went all your life and never let your Maker show you what was hidden in the cloisters?

You haven't made it this far into this study because you have an aversion to words, particularly if you've participated in the recordkeeping. You obviously have an affection for the words of Scripture and make room in your life and in your brain for reading other resources that could build your faith and expand your love for Jesus. In a social media age doing its best to reduce our concentration level to single-digit seconds, you've managed to be a reader. In my thinking, anyone who's willing to read as much as you do is able, either naturally or with enough practice, to write thoughtfully.

I think you have it in you—that well deep within, rich as oil, looking for a safe place to surface. To spill. To splash. To soak the floor. I think you have things to say. Things you wish you could find a way to say. Oh, you've lived some stories, haven't you? Good ones. Meaningful ones. Also heartrending ones. Baffling ones. Sad ones. Hard ones. Absurd ones. You don't ever have to tell them to anyone if you don't want to. But if you'll tell them to Jesus, in time he'll tell them back to you with the penlight of redemption. Perhaps you're wondering: Why tell him what he already knows? So he can tell you what he knows about your stories that you don't.

If you'll tell your stories to Jesus, in time he'll tell them back to you with the penlight of redemption.

The psalter is home to the best writing tutors in the biblical canon. In session 3, we noted that Psalms 1–41 are primarily penned by David. The songs and poems of Korah and Asaph unfold in Psalms 42–72 and are attributed almost exclusively to them in Psalms 73–89. Two psalms are credited to Solomon, and one each to Moses, Heman, and Ethan. Around forty-eight are anonymous. We're going to invite two psalms that are immense treasures to also be our teachers today. Both are psalms of the sons of Korah, and neither is especially lengthy. **Read Psalm 42 and Psalm 84.**

How are the beginnings of each psalm similar?

What seems to be the mood of each psalm?

Psalm 42	Psalm 84

If you had to guess, what kinds of things do you imagine prompted Psalm 42 and Psalm 84?

Psalm 42	Psalm 84

To whom is each psalm addressed?

Psalm 42	Psalm 84

Record any kind of imagery used in each psalm.

Psalm 42	Psalm 84

Which single verse in each psalm is most beautiful to you or fell on you most poignantly? Fill in the reference then write the verse beneath it.

Psalm 42: ________

Psalm 84:________

I love imagining the Spirit's process for moving the pens of the various psalmists. Did the lines come in bits and pieces or all at once, I wonder. Did the writers memorize the poems before they shared them? Were they satisfied the first time with what they'd written, or did they scratch them out and go at them again? Did they sing them? Hum them? Play them on an instrument? Some of the occasions are written into the verses. Other poems are general enough to serve as all-purpose songs of praise and petition.

To my hearing, both selections allude to stories written between the lines. Psalm 84 is a song of pilgrimage inviting the hearer on the long, arduous, and marvelous journey from the singer's home to God's own. The scenes on the journey are artfully woven to draw our feet into the yarn. We close our eyes and picture the landscapes painted with such familiar imagery that we nod. Yes, we've been there. We know what it's like to pass through the Valley of Baca—the Valley of Tears—and, if we're willing to sip the grace of our unseeable guide, in time our tears could turn to springs.

Here we are, you and I, in one piece, yearning to walk with God. After all we've each been through, our desire betrays that we, too, despite what we felt at the time, have gone "from strength to strength" on our way to the place God dwells. Can you picture just now some of those places you've been? Valleys of Tears? Fresh springs? Autumn rains arriving with blessings while you steadied yourself against the fierce wind blowing the leaves from the branches? Can you see yourself back there in that place, knowing that when you had nothing left to give, no blood left to bleed, you were supplied with new strength? **What is the first place that comes to your mind?**

Those valleys, tears, springs, and strengths all whisper bits and pieces of your very good story. What might happen if you turned up the volume so you could hear them? Then, if they refused to quit talking, what would you have to lose if you wrote some of them down? They speak of your adventures—perilous, precious, and unrepeatable. You may tell me adventures are only for the brave, and I will tell you only the brave stay willing to walk with God. After all, there's Psalm 42.

My tears have been my food day and night.

Why, my soul, are you so dejected?

I will say to God, my rock, "Why have you forgotten me?"

Haven't we known this breadth of experience? Haven't we basked in our God as sun and shield, feeling favored, honored, and blessed? Haven't we also wondered where God absconded and left us relentlessly hounded by disappointment? There you have it, the journey of faith. Given enough time, it takes every traveler to the extremities of feeling favored and forsaken, each finding its place in transport from glory to glory. In a way, the seasons of perceived forsakenness are intervals of divine favor disguised. Only there do we have the chance to choose faith over feeling. There, where emotion, sight, and circumstance conspire to make God seem traitorous, our faith is proved true.

When my father was in his late seventies, he gave each of my siblings and me a stack of pages blackened with single-spaced type he'd put through a copier and stapled on the top left corner. It was his story, he said proudly, from birth to present. Tyrannically taught to be polite, we each no doubt voiced some measure of gratitude. Sadly, I don't think one of us gave it a serious look until long after he was gone. His infidelities, betrayals, and abuses caused our family so much suffering, most of us wouldn't crack it open for years. **Has anyone ever caused enough havoc in your life that you'd find it similarly difficult to read something they'd written?**

My husband, Keith, read my father's writing first and told me how insightful it was. He was annoyingly insistent that I let him read bits and pieces to me. Months later, I set the coverless autobiography out where it would harass me into reading it, and in several sittings, I started and finished it. A detail about his childhood caught my eye. It was crowded in rapid-fire succession with others and written in the same cheerful tone of all that came before and after. Few things characterized my dad more consistently in my view than his detachment from any emotion appropriate to the moment.

Dad grew up poor in rural Arkansas, and his dad hunted rabbits and squirrels like many other men looking to put food on the table. Naturally, he took his son, my dad, along with him. Dad told almost in passing that he successfully begged his mom to keep him home because he hated killing the animals. Many pages later, with no obvious link to his previous aversion, he recounted his military career covering two wars and a span of twenty years. My dad was an artillery man.

I have no idea if all the shooting, the faraway and face-to-face, broke something in my dad. What I do know is that my father's story in his own words helped me see the man beyond the context of our leaky roof and cracked foundation. He had a bigger life than the one in which he'd bankrupted our respect. I'm glad he left us his story.

I have a dear friend who lost her marriage, her home, and her relationships with her adult children to the ravages of severe alcoholism. Sorrowfully, she may never get to meet her grandchildren. Advanced in age, she's haunted by the realistic fear of running out of time before they're ready to give her one more chance. I've pleaded with her to write her story. Without a hint of embellishment, what she's lived is the stuff of movies.

She asked, "If I did, would you keep it?"

"Oh, I surely would." And I will. "And I will treasure it and marvel over all you've endured." These thoughts cheered her, but I knew she wished for more than that. "And if I outlive you," I promised, "I will do my best to see that it someday falls into your grandchildren's hands."

Here is what I think or, Lord help me, what I hope: When they are old enough, mature enough, experienced enough to collect their own scars, they will hold it dear.

Each of us is so much more than our worst seasons and most terrible mistakes. Our lives are more than one role. Larger than one set of four walls.

I think you should write. That's what I'm trying to say. Even if you think no one would read what you have to say. Maybe the person who needs to read what you have to say is *you*. Because maybe you don't realize how much Jesus would show up in it. You wouldn't be on the other side of this page aching to walk nearer to him if he hadn't. Get out of your head that your story is one long, indecipherable smear of dark ink. "There is a river," the sons of Korah wrote in Psalm 46:4, as a glad intrusion when the earth gives way and mountains crash into seas. That river of God courses through your chapters with the red ink of redemption.

Write to Jesus. Write about Jesus. Write because of Jesus. Write about life. What you've seen. What you've felt. What you know to be true. What you fear. What you hope for. Who you've loved. Write phrases. Incomplete thoughts. Sentences strewn here and there. Paragraphs. Prayers. Letters. Lyrics. And somewhere along the way, but not too very late, think of writing your story.

Your truest story, the one in which you are neither hero nor villain. You are human. A human walking with God.

DAY 5

Do you not know? Have you not heard?

ISAIAH 40:21

One must forget many clichés in order to behold a single image.

ABRAHAM JOSHUA HESCHEL, *THE PROPHETS*

We meet today for our final lesson on "The Heart of Walking." If not for knowing the Gospels await us in Week 4, I'd say this farewell has come too soon. We have a marvelous place to go today that builds a bridge sturdy enough to cross from the Old Testament to the New. Allow me to introduce it with a riddle. What chapters of the Bible are thick with poetry but none to be found in the psalter? The answer? The books of the classical prophets.

Turn the pages of your Bible to the end of Song of Songs or Song of Solomon, depending on which name your translation assigns it. Hold your left hand there and turn to the final page of the Old Testament, just before Matthew, and place your right hand there. In the enormous section of Scripture between your palms, you hold the Major and Minor Prophets. While the book of Daniel is found in this section of our Christian Bibles, the Hebrew Bible places it among the *Ketuvim* (Writings), rather than the *Nevi'im* (Prophets).

The Hebrew Bible also counts Joshua, Judges, and the books of Samuel and Kings among the Nevi'im. In our copies of Scripture, however, you can consider the thick stack of Scripture you held between your hands as the classical prophets. Isaiah is the first we meet, and if not for Jeremiah's capacity to hold his own, Isaiah would've been a hard act to follow. The book's wide girth measures an impressive sixty-six chapters, almost as many as Matthew, Mark, and Luke combined.

Isaiah is penned in broad strokes, engaging three historical time periods for God's people: before, during, and after exile. It also spans a theological range virtually unmatched by any other book in the Bible. Unroll the scroll in its entirety, and from an aerial view, you'd see references to the very brackets of time: the original creation and the new creation. You'd find the Lord holding court, issuing indictments, warnings, judgments, and destructions. You'd also witness God comforting his people with unabashed maternal affection and calming the fretful with renewed promises.

The writing style is among its mesmerizing trademarks. The prophet's turn of pen is apparent from the beginning. **Look at Isaiah 1:1-2. What difference do you see between the formatting of verse one and verse two?**

Flip quickly through the pages of Isaiah, but attentively enough to note the predominant format. Aside from the narrative portions in chapters 6–8 and 36–39, the book of Isaiah is written almost entirely in poetry. Most of the classical prophets are! We often open the books of the prophets in dread, expecting crusty old, wild-eyed, wiry-haired curmudgeons, and to our surprise, discover poets. Sometimes wild-eyed, wiry-haired curmudgeon-poets, but poets nonetheless. And, so, we're left with another riddle, but one we mortals cannot answer: Did God make prophets of poets or poets of prophets?

The big question begging to be asked is this: Why so much poetry from the pens of prophets? Ultimately only the Lord can answer the question, but surely one reason is for love of verse—the beauty, the parallelism, the rhythm, the liberty of song to get a message across. Prophetic poetry employs images, creates scenes, and conveys emotions often bigger than life to grab the attention of the reader, to warn, awaken, and also to reassure. One could argue that God means to terrify his people into repentance through the prophets. That's not to say the threats were empty. They weren't. But poetry is meant to stretch the imagination into engagement, especially where hearts have grown dull to the facts.

Scholar Katie M. Heffelfinger, referencing a portion of Isaiah, describes divine speech presented poetically this way:

> [Poetry is] a form that conveys truth in a way that problematizes our affection for simplicity. Biblical poetry invokes and glories in complexity. It renders truth rich and full by embracing the ambiguity inherent in human experience, by intensifying

our encounter with the emotional element of our grasping truth, and by holding competing truths in juxtaposed and realistic tension.[10]

What part of Dr. Heffelfinger's explanation makes the most sense to you?

By now you're ready to read from Isaiah rather than simply talk about it. So am I. **Please read Isaiah 63:7–64:12 for a bridge from places we've been in our study to the Gospels we will crack open next week.**

How did God respond to the suffering of his people in Isaiah 63:9?

What did God "remember," according to Isaiah 63:11?

What does Isaiah 64:7 say no one was doing?

And yet what was still true, according to Isaiah 64:8?

Reread Isaiah 64:11. What had happened to their "holy and beautiful temple"?

The persistent waywardness of God's people despite repeated divine warnings had ironically given them what they'd demanded. Crudely put, God was saying something like this. *You want their gods? Have them. You want their kings? Have them. Go right ahead. See how it goes.* It went just as it typically does when people who bear the Lord's name decide to play the world's game:

- The people of God become enamored by the empire (loss of perspective).
- Then they became enveloped by the empire (loss of distinctiveness).
- Then they were exploited by the empire (loss of freedom).

The words of Isaiah 63:19 are loaded. **Fill in the blanks and reflect on them.**

"We have become like ________________________________

________________________, like ________________________

____."

We can so badly want God to be Victor, Defender, Deliverer, Healer, Miracle Worker, and Provider, but not our Ruler. We want blessing, not bossing. Our natural inclination is to want to be Potter, and God, the clay.

Then four words tumble out in Isaiah 64:1 that, if allowed to seep into our pores and get under our skin, can be as sore to the touch as a deep-purple bruise. They are familiar to most who have been on this journey of faith for long—sometimes hauntingly so: "If only you would . . ."

Do you hear the vulnerability? Can you hear the song shift into a high-pitched chord of desperation? Can you sense something akin to childlikeness? If you're like me, you have raised those four words to God at some of the scariest, most foreboding, demoralizing moments of your life.

- If only you would heal . . .
- If only you would put a stop this . . .
- If only you would intervene . . .
- If only you would command that addiction to be broken . . .

- If only you would fix this marriage . . .
- If only you would take me home . . .

What has been one of your most memorable times of "God, if only you would . . ."?

I'd imagine we could all recount times we've cried out to heaven, "If only you would . . ." and he has. And we've also pleaded, "If only you would . . ." and he hasn't. Don't imagine for a moment those are faithless words. Those the prophet speaks for have been brought to such a low place of consequence and divine discipline, they can see with their own eyes how their idols have failed them. Notice how they don't say, "If only you could . . ." but "If only you *would*. . ." Faith knows he can. Hopelessness assumes he won't.

What exactly are the people asking God, "If only you would . . ."? (Isaiah 64:1).

The Israelites are pining for Sinai. Pining for thick dark clouds, blazing fire, claps of thunder, and bolts of lightning. They are pleading, "Take us back to the exodus! Do it again! Come down that same way, with that same power and wonder. Show off to our enemies like you did back then!"

Psalm 137, a song of the exiles, sings a fitting refrain from this same frame of mind. **Read Psalm 137:1-4. Where were the exiles at the time?**

What had they done with their harps, and why?

What was their question in Psalm 137:4?

Why this weeping "by the rivers of Babylon" while they remembered Zion? My guess is they yearned for God to part the waters as he did in Exodus when he delivered the Hebrew slaves from Egypt and, perhaps more pointedly, as he did again in Joshua when he parted the Jordan River to deliver the Israelites to the Promised Land. This, in essence, is the cry in Isaiah 64:

> You who came down, come down again! Do what you did before!

Strangely, it was this very expectation God was calling to account when he said through the prophet Isaiah,

> "Do not remember the past events;
> pay no attention to things of old.
> Look, I am about to do something new;
> even now it is coming. Do you not see it?
> Indeed, I will make a way in the wilderness,
> rivers in the desert.
>
> ISAIAH 43:18-19

God's point? Quit expecting a repeat performance. The Lord is Deliverer and will not cease to deliver but reserves the right to do it any way he pleases.

How has he delivered you before? Have you—as I have, at times—hung up your harp and parked yourself on the shore, watching for him to do the same thing, the same way as before? Or how about this one: Have you ever been suspicious of another person's journey to greater freedom or deeper wholeness because it differed from yours? Oh, I have. When I first tasted some actual liberty in Christ, I somehow had it in my head that everyone's journey into the Scriptures or out of their bondage would look similar to mine. Boy, was I wrong.

Can you relate to any of the questions in this paragraph? If so, how?

Note how God flips the script in Isaiah 43:19. Formerly he'd put a strip of desert in the river so they could cross over to the promise on dry ground. In Isaiah the Lord says, "Forget that! This time I will deliver you to the promise through strips of water dividing the desert."

We can be so sure how God works based on our interpretations of the past that we miss a new work right under our noses. God is not a magician. There's no bag of tricks. God is so much greater. So much more. He's the Lord, the Creator of heaven and earth, the Commander of land and sea. God speaks, and it is so. Nothing is too difficult for him. Nothing is out of reach. Sometimes the miracle we need is more imagination.

Read Isaiah 64:1-5 a final time:

If only you would tear the heavens open
and come down,
so that mountains would quake at your presence—
just as fire kindles brushwood,
and fire boils water—
to make your name known to your enemies,
so that nations would tremble at your presence!
When you did awesome works
that we did not expect,
you came down,
and the mountains quaked at your presence.
From ancient times no one has heard,
no one has listened to,
no eye has seen any God except you
who acts on behalf of the one who waits for him.
You welcome the one who joyfully does what is right;
they remember you in your ways.
But we have sinned, and you were angry.
How can we be saved if we remain in our sins?

How indeed?

The Lord responded affirmatively to their plea, "If only you would . . . come down." He *would* come down, but not with flash and fire this time. No voice sounding like a trumpet. No thunder. No public proclamation, except to a handful of shepherds keeping watch over their flocks by night. He'd come down in otherwise absolute obscurity. No one made room for this. There was no trembling mountain. Instead, a trembling young mother. There were no priests or prophets. Instead, a virgin giving birth. God would break the sound barrier through the cries of a newborn babe, wrapped in swaddling clothes, come to save the world.

Though this very one had been foretold by Isaiah, most of God's people had no room in the lodgings of their minds for him to come—not just down, but so very far, so deeply down, humbling himself "by assuming the form of a servant, taking on the likeness of humanity . . . becoming obedient to the point of death—even to death on a cross" (Philippians 2:7-8).

For every "O God, if only you would . . ." there is a *could* we'd never imagine.

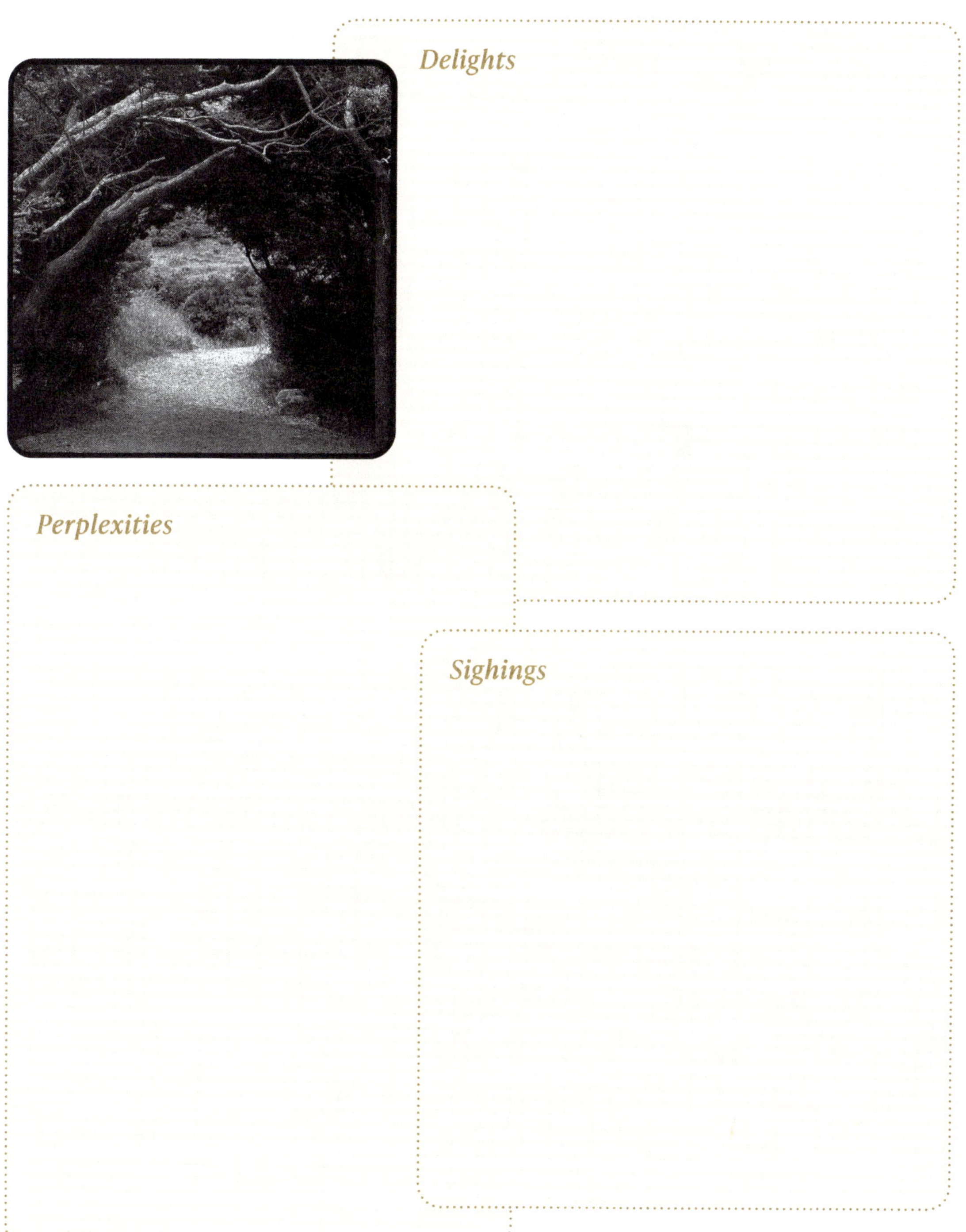

Delights

Perplexities

Sighings

Laments

Word Alerts

Divine Consolations/Comforts

Perceived Presence

WEEK 4

the DISCIPLESHIP *of* WALKING

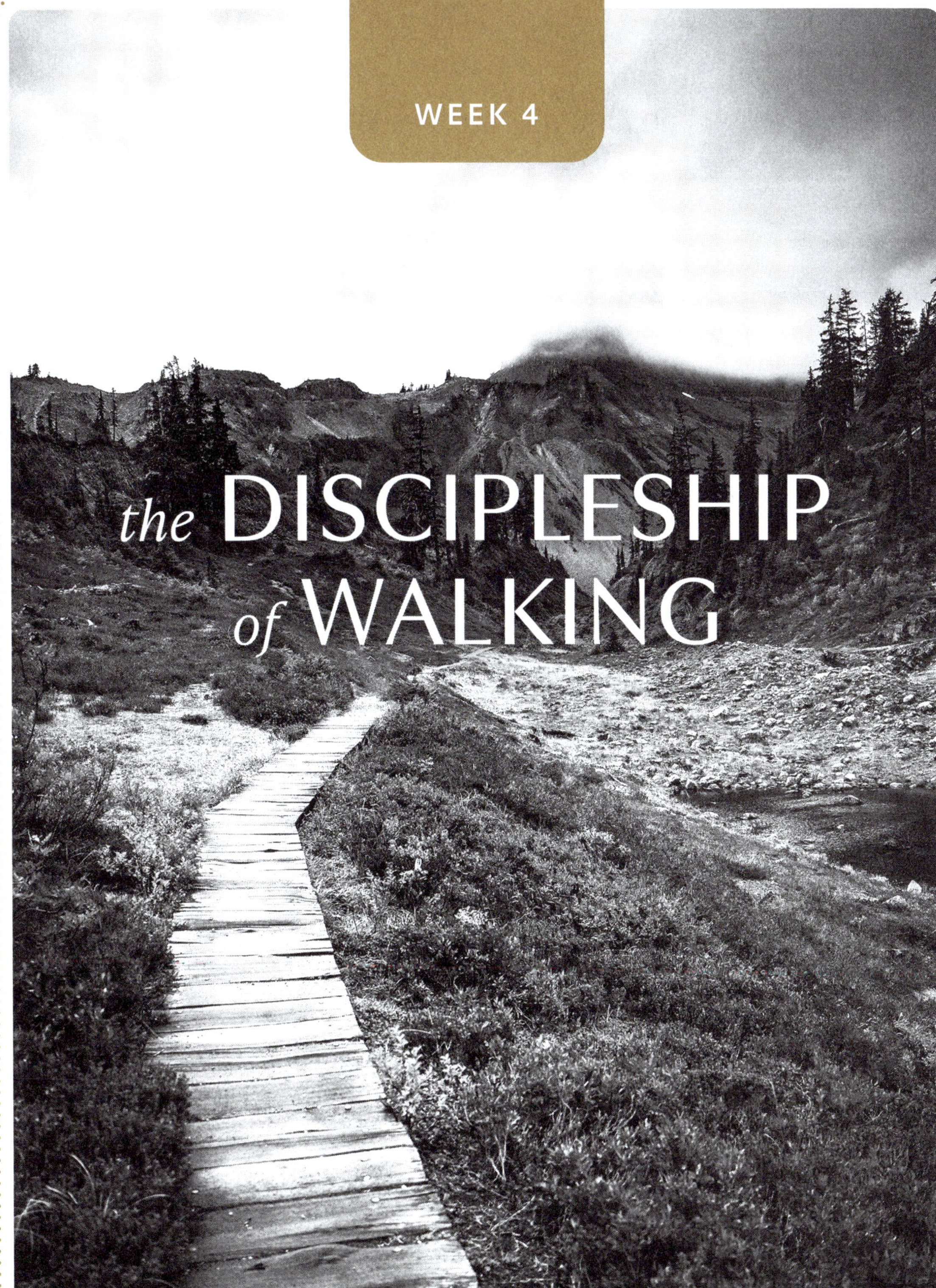

SESSION 4

The Discipleship of Walking

You can fill in these blanks as you watch the video for session 4.

Introduction: In our present series, we're preoccupying ourselves with one concept: walking with God. We're pursuing various angles of humans like us walking with God in unfolding eras of biblical history. Thus far, we've focused on "The Beginning of Walking" in Genesis, "The Law of Walking" in the Books of Moses, and last week, we searched "The Heart of Walking" amid the hymns and liturgies of the psalmists. Today we crack open the Gospels to seek out the ____________________ of walking.

We'll lay the foundation for today's angle on walking with God with the following texts:

1. John 1:29-46: Note the contagion effect of ________________________.
2. 1 John 1:1-7; 2:6
3. Hebrews 10:1-10

A suggestion of one word to encapsulate a whole category of Christ's disciple-making:

_______________ . . .

For _______________

For _______________

For _______________

For _______________ the _______________

For _______________

For _______________

For _______________

For _______________

For _______________

For _______________

For _______, _______, _______ (aka___, ___, _______)

For _______________

For _______________

For _______________

For _______________

*Video session available for purchase at **TyndaleChristianResources.com**.*

Welcome to week 4! A heads-up before we begin today's lesson: Day 3 of this week and next week (our final week) are each set aside for you to interview a person about their walk with God. If you've watched any of the interviews I conducted as bonus material for this study, including this week's interview with Ray and Jani Ortlund, you know the kinds of questions I asked, but you get to freestyle any way you please.* It's your interview! You'll find that I've supplied questions if you prefer, but skip any you please, tweak others according to your interests, or mark them out and write in your own. Here are a few recommendations regarding each of your interviewees:

- Choose reachable people whose walk with God you find authentic and, for any number of reasons, admirable. The goal is to complete these interviews before our study ends, so accessibility is key.
- Conduct the interviews using whatever method works best for you and your interviewee. For example, you can supply the questions by email and request written responses. You can meet in person, by phone, or on screen, jotting down their responses in real time or, depending upon the person's comfort level, using your phone recorder and filling in the answers afterward. If your interviewee requests the questions in advance, by all means, supply them.
- Respect your interviewee's time. This is an enormous key to success. I asked each of my guests for exactly one hour, and no matter how tempted I was to continue the conversation, I made myself honor it.
- Enjoy them! I have no doubt they will enjoy you.

*  *Find Beth's interview with Ray and Jani Ortlund here.*

NOTES

DAY 1

By his death, Jesus opened a new and life-giving way through the curtain into the Most Holy Place.

HEBREWS 10:20, NLT

On the day called Sunday, all who live in cities or in the country gather together to one place, and the memoirs of the apostles or the writings of the prophets are read, as long as time permits.

JUSTIN MARTYR, *FIRST APOLOGY*

An author of my delicate age knows that if you want to put nails in your coffin as someone who cares to be read, just use dated illustrations and figures of speech. The problem is, I've found no adequate replacement for the expression my elementary school teachers used with abandon to preface a lesson requiring rapt attention. "Okay, students, you're going to need to put on your thinking caps."

Whatever the teacher said for the next sixty seconds was lost on me because I became preoccupied with putting on my thinking cap. I pictured it to the minutest detail. It was shaped more like a beanie than a cap, so it fit right on top of my brain instead of leaving space like a baseball cap would do. This stylistic touch could only help. Outdated or not, go up in your attic, find your grandmother's thinking cap, and stick it on your head. You may need it today.

This week we move to our fourth biblical era to search out "The Discipleship of Walking." Joyously, this shift to the New Testament plants our feet squarely in the Gospels. We've already taken this leap by way of video session 4 in the magnificent Gospel of John. His was likely the last of the Gospels written. **Take a moment to compare the lengths of all four Gospels. How many chapters are found in each book?**

Matthew ____________________

Mark ________________________

Luke ________________________

John ________________________

Though Mark appears second among the four in the New Testament, most scholars believe it was penned first, a prospect you'll hopefully find increasingly significant through the lesson. We're singling out Mark's Gospel for a proper introduction because it has a marvelous way of introducing the others. As you noted above, his Gospel is far and away the briefest, but light on words doesn't mean light on theology. God strategically placed this writer under the tutelage of the most remarkable leaders and teachers in the early church.

The book is traditionally attributed to John Mark, the son of a woman named Mary. Yes, Mary. I like the name and all. It's just that one might wonder (namely, yours truly) why so many women in the Bible shared the same name. The Hebrew men, after all, had for centuries answered to a wide assortment of names. Take Isaiah's son by his wife, the prophetess, in Isaiah 8:3. His name was Maher-shalal-hash-baz. And Jonathan's son Mephibosheth. Try calling those kids in for supper. In case you, too, can hardly get through a phrase in Scripture without asking questions, you might be blessed to have this matter settled. Mary is the Greek equivalent to the Hebrew name Miriam, Moses' sister and a hero to Jewish women. As many as one in four Jewish baby girls in the first century answered to her name.

John Mark's mother, some five Marys in, finds a place of no small significance in the early church, because her home is one of the first places outside a synagogue we find Christians gathered after the Day of Pentecost (Acts 12:12). Perhaps the entire extended family had financial standing, since Mark was also a cousin of Barnabas, a devout Jesus-follower and a major benefactor of the church in Jerusalem. Paul and Barnabas took him on their first missionary journey, but for reasons we're not told, he dropped out of the trip early. Barnabas wanted to take his cousin on their second journey too. **According to Acts 15:39, how did Paul feel about the prospect, and why?**

Mark became the bone of contention that broke a fruitful partnership into pieces. That Mark won back the confidence of Paul is beautifully and refreshingly clear in the apostle's final letter. "Bring Mark with you," he instructed Timothy, "for he is useful to me in the ministry" (2 Timothy 4:11). Mark's most consequential relationship in terms of the gospel, however, was with Peter. They shared a bond that was no doubt forged by the Holy Spirit. **First Peter 5:13 may hold some fascinating clues to Mark's Gospel. Write the verse in this space:**

Babylon is almost certainly symbolic for Rome. As Dr. Thomas R. Schreiner writes, "Peter drew on Old Testament tradition, where Babylon represents those opposed to God. . . . In this instance, as in Revelation (17–18), Babylon designates Rome itself, the enemy of God."[1]

This is where things get particularly interesting regarding Mark's Gospel. Since the Bible doesn't supply clear references to Mark as an eyewitness to the life of Jesus, where did he get his information? Peter, who could hardly have had a closer view, is believed to be his source. Mark may have received Peter's account in Rome during the apostle's imprisonment and pending martyrdom. This prospect is particularly intriguing in view of the urgency with which Mark wrote.

The Gospel of Mark gallops out of the gate like a horse in a race, the heart of its rider pounding with holy passion. You'll quickly notice he takes no pause for a birth narrative, like Matthew and Luke do. Instead, his pen flies like the wind toward the crucifixion. Fittingly, this Gospel is famous for its roughly forty occurrences of the Greek adverb *euthys*, often translated "immediately." *Euthys* appears eleven times in the first chapter alone. The repetition throughout the book escalates the drama and, in the words of Dr. W. W. Wessel, "gives his Gospel a certain air of breathlessness."[2]

Now we're ready to read Mark 1:1-11. After completing the reading, return to verse 1 and write it in this space:

At first blush, Mark's opening words don't seem very moving, but they serve as a prologue bursting wide open with meaning. By the Holy Spirit's design, Genesis 1:1; John 1:1; and Mark 1:1 in their original languages all start with *the beginning*. Let that sink in a bit. You'll seldom hear a sermon or teaching on John 1:1 that doesn't make the connection to Genesis 1:1. Both speak of beginnings in the context of creation. Mark 1:1 could well be considered in that same mix.

- Genesis 1:1 references creation.
- John 1:1 references pre-creation.
- Mark 1:1 references new creation.

According to scholar James R. Edwards, "For Mark the introduction of Jesus is no less momentous than the creation of the world, for in Jesus a new creation is at hand."[3]

With this thought in mind, **reread Mark 1:2-3**. Mark means the reader to grasp that the ushering in of this good news is no detour or backup plan. Rather, it is the fulfillment of Scripture, all the way down to a forerunner who would be an Elijah-like prophet. Here Mark takes a portion of Exodus 23:20 and Malachi 3:1 as well as Isaiah 40:3 in full and braids them into one strand. In the words of Isaiah, the prince among Israel's prophets, even the wilderness reference sprouts with meaning.

Mark makes clear, as do the other Gospel writers, that John baptized people for a purpose that differed from the baptism Christ would bring. **What was the nature of John's more provisional baptism (Mark 1:4-5)?**

How was John's faithfulness to his task of preparing the way made beautifully evident in Mark 1:7?

Look attentively at the scene Mark 1:9-11 captures for us. Matthew and John offer details we don't find in this account of Christ's baptism. Luke's record is brief like Mark's, but remember, fewer words don't indicate smaller theological thoughts. In both the opening sentence of Mark's Gospel and his account of the baptism, the emphasis is on Jesus the Christ (or Messiah) as the anointed Son of God, incomparably loved by the Father and utterly pleasing to him.

You might be fascinated to know that, while Matthew and Luke report heaven being opened (*anoigein*), Mark alone notes "the heavens being torn (*schizein*) open." A corresponding term used in the Old Testament for this effect is the Hebrew *qara*, meaning "to tear." Is this perchance ringing a bell from our previous lesson? Guess where we find this corresponding Hebrew word?

> If only you would tear the heavens open and come down . . .
>
> ISAIAH 64:1

Remember when we talked about Mark writing his Gospel like a man in a hurry? With a gallop driven by immediacy? A dozen chapters pass in a dramatic flurry, then something conspicuous happens when Mark gets to the narrative of Jesus' passion. He suddenly leans back, pulls hard on the reins, and slows that steed to a walk. As N. Clayton Croy, professor of New Testament, points out (specifically with reference to Mark 14:1–15:47), "This is the climax of the drama, and a more deliberate pace is appropriate, even in this swiftly moving gospel. . . . Mark devotes two chapters (one hundred and nineteen verses) to the period from Jesus' anointing at Bethany to his burial in a rock hewn tomb, giving strikingly detailed coverage for this forty-eight to sixty hour period of Jesus' life."[4]

Can you think of a time when you hurried to a certain spot so you could slow down and take it in? Imagine taking a friend on a road trip to the most fascinating place you've ever been. Maybe someone took you there a little while ago, and you can't shake it out of your head. You're compelled to go back with an urgency you hardly understand, and this time you're taking another person with you. She loads up in the passenger seat and throws her baggage in the back seat, and you hop behind the wheel. You're taking the scenic route, but for the first couple of hours, you keep the accelerator pressed to the floor.

The sights flying past the open windows are mesmerizing enough to your passenger that she asks why you aren't stopping *here* . . . and *there* . . . and *Would you look at that? Shouldn't we pull over there?* You agree. The whole trip is a marvel. But you have a destination on your mind. A place she's never seen. A fearsome place. A disturbing place. A place where darkness descends eerily early, and thunder roars, and you have to hold tight to a nearby tree as the earth quakes beneath your feet. A place of horrors. A place of wonders. A place where the dead die slowly. Then a place where the dead go missing.

You know where you're headed. She doesn't. Then suddenly, you see the clouds collecting ahead. You throw on the brakes, pull over in the gravel, turn off the ignition, and say to her, "Let's walk from here." That's how it was for Mark, I think: making haste to the place where he wanted to slow down.

Life is moving fast, isn't it? Flying by, the colors blurring in your periphery, people's faces less and less recognizable. Everything's changing at such a rapid pace, you wonder if the technology you're learning today will be obsolete tomorrow. You were a little girl once upon a time when time was not in such a rush. You loved stories. Make-believe. And books that made you believe. You long for that feeling again. That swept-up feeling when a north wind blows with someplace to go and the ceiling disappears and the walls of your small room fall open like four cards from a paper-thin deck. And there it is—a world beyond your imagination. A world of grim villains and real heroes and high stakes and low blows. A story so much bigger than yours that you know, if you loosen your grip on all you've relied on and ride the wings of this wind, you might well get lost. You let go and give way.

And along the way, you realize this is no fairy tale at all, and the story you risked being lost within is true. Then, after all you've seen, felt, and heard, the wind slows and your feet land and you find yourself once more in a room, only this time it's a strange room: lamp lit, shadows lurking, the smell of incense burning, and the walls closing in on you. You stand before a heavy curtain with no seam. You're startled by a sound that starts at the ceiling.

Don't move a muscle. Remember that word Mark used in 1:10 when he described Jesus coming up from the waters of baptism? "He saw the heavens being torn open."

Torn open. Just like Israel had prayed, but nothing like Israel had pictured. *If only you would tear the heavens open . . .*

Mark only uses the word *schizein* ("to tear") one more time in his Gospel. You'll want to slow to a crawl and see this for yourself. I've already invited you into the room. You know the one I'm talking about: where shadows leap and lurch and your eyes burn from the smoke of the incense. We've snuck in, you may as well know, because the room is set apart for men only—priests only—and just one at a time. But I won't tell, if you don't.

Read Mark 15:37-39 and catch your breath as Jesus breathes his last. Steady yourself at the deafening sound of the heavy veil rending, hooks to hem, the old script ripping in two. Gather your courage and gird up your garments. Walk through the tear in the curtain to a new and living way. Gaze upon the mercy seat there between the cherubim. Be quiet. Be still. Just listen. Hear the echo of a centurion's voice reverberating from a hill not so far away:

> Truly this man was the Son of God!
>
> MARK 15:39

DAY 2

Whoever has ears, let them hear.

MATTHEW 11:15, NIV

You saw him, I dare say, up yonder. He was, and is yet, most likely, the wearisomest self-righteous pharisee that ever ransacked a Bible to rake the promises to himself and fling the curses on his neighbours.

EMILY BRONTË, *WUTHERING HEIGHTS*

Open your Bible to Matthew 13. Elbow your way into a large crowd gathered on the shore of the Galilean Sea and stand shoulder to shoulder with the spectators in front. You won't need long to spot the center of attention. Jesus has climbed into a boat far enough from the water's edge to be visible to those assembled but close enough to be heard. Hold your position for a few moments of background from Matthew's Gospel to explain the size of the crowd. His reputation as a miracle worker was based on far more than rumor. Matthew 4:23-25 reads,

> He went throughout all Galilee, teaching in their synagogues and proclaiming the gospel of the kingdom and healing every disease and every affliction among the people. So his fame spread throughout all Syria, and they brought him all the sick, those afflicted with various diseases and pains, those oppressed by demons, those having seizures, and paralytics, and he healed them. And great crowds followed him from Galilee and the Decapolis, and from Jerusalem and Judea, and from beyond the Jordan.
>
> MATTHEW 4:23-25, ESV

At that time, only Peter, Andrew, James, and John had been summoned by Jesus to follow him. Imagine the crash course in discipleship these small-town fishermen received. They'd known the losses, pain, sickness, and death characteristic of any village in their region, but they'd never seen such a convulsive sea of suffering humanity. Even in our screen-driven culture, with video access to a mind-bending spectrum of tragedies and traumas, few of us have ever stood arm's length from throngs of people stricken with disease, debilitating pain, seizures, paralysis, and demonic oppression.

Put yourself there in your mind's eye alongside Peter, Andrew, James, and John. All your senses are abruptly awakened to the sights, scents, and sounds of the afflicted coming to Jesus in droves. And then watch him heal them. One by one, each made well. What would you do with the whiplash of tragedy and triumph? With that kind of induction into ministry, imagine trying to sleep at night. Think how we'd whisper to one another in the dark, "Did you see that?"

The next scene in Matthew involves another crowd, only this time Jesus sits down on a hillside and his disciples join him. "He began to teach them, saying: 'Blessed are the poor in spirit, for the kingdom of heaven is theirs'" (Matthew 5:2-3). That the follow-up sermon to their shockingly widened world is the Sermon on the Mount is the furthest thing from coincidence. In a message stretching three chapters wide in the wordy Gospel of Matthew, Jesus teaches the values of the Kingdom of God, where virtually every worldly perception of success and righteousness is turned upside down (heaven's view of earth) and inside out (the heart beneath the claims).

The intervening chapters in Matthew include an array of more detailed miracles, as well as the commissioning, empowering, and sending forth of the twelve apostles. We have enough background now to return to our positions in Matthew 13, shoulder to shoulder with the crowd on the seashore, focused on a bearded man about thirty years old telling stories from a boat.

Read Matthew 13:1-23 with your initial focus on the parable and its interpretation. If you're familiar with the story, ask God to help you view it with fresh eyes and a receptive heart. How would you capture the overall point of the parable in one sentence or phrase?

In the seed sown along the path, Jesus indicates the evil one has a capacity we probably don't take seriously enough (verse 19). **What is it?**

Instantaneous joy is a marvelous reaction to the words of Christ, but in the seed sown on rocky ground (verses 20-21), we discover that a surge of joy—in and of itself—isn't sustaining. **Why is that?**

The seed sown among the thorns (verses 7 and 22) illustrates a truth we'll never master so thoroughly we won't need to hear it again. The next big crisis is all it takes to forget it. **Record the meaning of the seed sown among thorns:**

What constitutes good ground, according to verse 23?

If we were to take this parable literally, how good of an investment is truly hearing the words about the Kingdom?

Now search Matthew 13:1-23 for any form of the word *understand*. How many times do you find it, and in which verses?

What seems to be its level of importance?

Jesus isn't saying we'll reach the point of completely understanding God or the whole canon of Scripture or Christ's words about the Kingdom in this lifetime. Our human minds are frustratingly finite. Books like Job, Psalms, Jeremiah, and Romans speak openly about the unsearchable and unfathomable mind of God. In Isaiah 55:8-9, God declares,

> For my thoughts are not your thoughts, and your ways are not my ways. . . .
> For as heaven is higher than earth, so my ways are higher than your ways.

Yet, interestingly, in that exact chapter of Scripture, God also speaks of the accomplishing aspect of divine words. They are depicted as seeds germinated by rain and snowfall from heaven, bringing forth purposeful harvests.

Here's the long and short of it: In matters pertaining to God, understanding at times amounts to understanding that some things can't be understood. Understanding may mean grasping with our minds that the ways of Jesus are good, right, true, and consistent with his self-revelation, even when our hearts feel betrayed by his will.

For now, look back at Matthew 13:9 and write it in this space:

Who came up to the teacher after the parable to ask a question (verse 10)?

Don't let it slip past you that "anyone who has ears" can listen. What a beautiful truth! Anyone within earshot or eyeshot of Christ's words is invited to become good soil for seed he promises will bear fruit. Notice, however, that only the disciples are on record coming up to Jesus afterward with a question. Others were presumably satisfied to take the story at face value. After all, farming could hardly have been more essential to their survival. The disciples, however, wanted to *understand*. They knew the lesson was about more than farming. They wanted to know what Jesus was really saying and why he was using a parable to say it. You see, face value is one thing. Faith value is another.

Face value is one thing. Faith value is another.

Here's the essential question the parable is placing on the desk of every student: What will we do with Christ's words? Not just any teacher's words. *Christ's* words. Those with the accomplishing power to bring the galaxies into existence ex nihilo. What will we do with his words?

The art of the parable is masterful in the Gospels. Sometimes Jesus uses story to simplify what seems complicated. Other times Jesus uses story to complicate what seems simple. The genius of the parable is how it requires something from the hearer. A certain amount of devotion is necessary for getting the point. Will the hearer listen to the end? Try to think any deeper? Attempt to make sense of the story beyond its face value? Who will stay after class to ask questions?

One of the largest obstacles to learning in the classroom of a great teacher is thinking we've already learned it. A child is naturally endued with curiosity. The shame is not in asking earnest questions. The shame is in outgrowing them. Curiosity is part of coming to Jesus as a child and, paradoxically, the only way to grow up.

Peruse Matthew 13:10-17, where Christ responds to the disciples' question, "Why are you speaking to them in parables?" What do you think he means in verse 12 by "Whoever has, more will be given to him"?

We can listen again and again to the words of Christ and never understand. We can stare unblinkingly at the page for hours on end yet never perceive. On the other hand, we can receive, ponder, believe, and treasure what seems to others the most elementary, shoulder-shrugging truth from Christ, and he'll reveal himself to us again. And again. And again.

The prophecy Jesus quotes in Matthew 13:14-15 was originally in reference to a people who believed they were too special and set apart for God to let them reap the disaster their corrupt hearts had sown. They were right to think that God is merciful. They were wrong to think that God is coddling. No position (in this case, that of Abraham's descendants) or place (Jerusalem or the Temple) would serve as a shelter. God is the shelter of his people, and bright is the light in his shadow.

Fast-forward some seven hundred years, and the crowds around Jesus are not so different. Fast-forward two millennia, and those of us crowding around Jesus' name still have the same tendencies. The temperature can go down on our hearts so slowly, we don't realize we've turned cold. The dimming of our sight so gradual, we're unaware how little we see. The cacophony so loud, we miss the still, small voice that, once upon a time, we lived to hear.

The impact of a calloused heart on artistry is titanic and often the last thing a person thinks to blame. Sometimes the culprit responsible for our creative block is our own hard heart, shutting in the gift. Vulnerability is essential to an artist in virtually any field. To block all possibility of wounding is to dry the paint.

Maybe you don't consider yourself an artist. Then again, maybe your gifting is too obvious to deny. But this much is true of us all: We are created in the image of one who is the essence and originator of all creativity. Bearing the thumbprint of your Maker means you possess some measure of creative flair that adds a splash of color to what you offer the world. Don't let it get trapped inside a hardened heart.

The loss of our spiritual senses isn't always accidental or gradual. **Detect the telling term in Matthew 13:15. Jesus didn't say the people were blind. He didn't say they could not see. He said, "They have ____________________ their eyes."** Some wrongs are so obvious, we'd have to press our palms to the lids of our eyes not to see them. Perhaps, like me, you can't fathom how chattel slave traders who tore babies from their mothers' breasts to auction the women off like cattle could live with themselves. Even a seared conscience seems to me an insufficient explanation of such obvious evil. Among the hosts of harm survivors of childhood sexual abuse are challenged to overcome, one of the most tormenting questions is whether relatives, teachers, or parents truly couldn't see the signs or shut their eyes. **Offer an example**

of your own in which it seems a person would have to purposely shut his or her eyes to keep from seeing the truth.

In Isaiah 6, where the prophecy Jesus quotes first appears, the bad news regarding callous hearts, unseeing eyes, and unhearing ears is purposely left hanging. Jesus, however, tags a new ending to the bewildering story: good news, indeed *gospel* news, planned from the start, its due date finally come. This good news was not only about those first disciples. It is also about us. **You'll find it in Matthew 13:15. What is it?**

I've saved our look at the meaningful word *understand* as our conclusion. **Circle it in Matthew 13:15 and underline the part of the verse following it.**

> This people's heart has grown callous; their ears are hard of hearing, and they have shut their eyes; otherwise they might see with their eyes, and hear with their ears, and understand with their hearts, and turn back—and I would heal them.

Contemplate the role understanding plays in the kind of healing Jesus conveys. In Matthew's context, healing is a result of arriving at an understanding that causes a person to turn from waywardness to God's way of saving through the Son. Read the definition of the word translated "understand" in Matthew 13:15 from this Greek dictionary and imagine the implications regarding a multitude of heart maladies.

> **συνίημι suníēmi**; from *sún*, together or together with, and *híēmi*, to send or put. To comprehend, understand, perceive. The comprehending activity of the mind denoted by *suníēmi* entails the assembling of individual facts into an organized whole, as collecting the pieces of a puzzle and putting them together. The mind grasps concepts and sees the proper relationship between them.[5]

Have you ever had a few puzzle pieces come together in your life that made you think maybe your existence wasn't a jumbled heap of random experiences after all? If so, what were they?

One gift God gave me through writing a memoir was putting a period on the final sentence, scooting my chair back, and realizing how a handful of experiences, encounters, and events that seemed to make no sense at all actually fit together in the overall scheme. The realization mended something in me. Not everything, of course, but enough to appreciate a few chapters of my story I'd so long despised.

An unexpected miracle can occur when you keep walking with God. You stop to pick up a random puzzle piece someone must have dropped in the dirt and you stick it in your pocket. A few miles down the road, another piece, half hidden under a leaf, catches your eye. You pick it up and study it and remember the one in your pocket. You pull it out and hold it next to the second one. *Wait a minute. They're pieces of the same puzzle? Adjacent pieces? How can this be?* What you don't realize is that Jesus is the one dropping them in the soil, half hidden so only a set of eyes that truly perceive can find them.

An unexpected miracle can occur when you keep walking with God.

Life's so puzzling, isn't it? *Why this? Why that?* So much doesn't make sense. But all it takes to make you suspect your Maker has been intentional in the path you've walked is finding a few pieces that fit. By faith, you somehow know that if God caused these seemingly random pieces to go together, one bright dawn the Teller of the everlasting story will spread them all out and put them together as one before your very eyes.

DAY 3

It's time for your interview with someone you respect about their walk with God. I've included sample questions here, but feel free to ask different questions, add to these, or change directions if something they say piques your interest.

Name:

Your relationship to the person:

Share a little about your childhood, particularly the dimensions that later impacted your walk with God, whether positively or negatively.

Were you involved in a church or any kind of community of faith in your upbringing? If so, tell me something about it.

How did you come to know Jesus?

Were you discipled in your early days of faith? If so, who were you discipled by, and what did that process look like? If not, how did you find your own way with Jesus?

The reason I wanted to interview you is because, from my observation, your walk with God conveys authenticity and bears obvious fruit. Many people who come to know Jesus might not choose to walk with him in the kind of closeness you seem to. **What caused you to want to walk consistently and closely with God?**

What is the biggest difference walking with God has made to you?

Share a little about what walking with God looks like for you in the day in, day out routine. I'd love to have insight into how you practice some spiritual disciplines like prayer and Scripture reading. **For example, how do you choose what segment you are going to read? Do you journal? I'd enjoy knowing about practices that nurture your walk with God.**

What are a few resources besides your Bible that you find enriching?

Have you had the joy of close companions in your walk of faith? If so, have they been the same people throughout your life, or did different seasons bring different individuals?

If you could give only one piece of advice to someone beginning their journey of faith, what would it be?

Without feeling pressure to sound deep, name two of your very favorite things about Jesus.

DAY 4

The God of peace will soon crush Satan under your feet.

ROMANS 16:20

Nobody knows the trouble I've seen
Nobody knows but Jesus.

NINETEENTH-CENTURY SPIRITUAL

All five weeks of our written work and each of our video sessions share one aim: observing what walking with God can look like. Today's lesson escorts us to the same destination but from a different side of the tracks. Mark's substantially shorter Gospel reserves a space of twenty verses to show us a life that had been bound by forces of darkness until the Light arrived. If you've ever wondered what the unleashed will of Satan could look like in a living human being, today's segment offers an unnerving example. File this lesson under the heading "If Satan Had His Way."

We'll start our reading a few verses earlier than the scene of our focus, because trouble was in the air before this encounter. Please read Mark 4:35-41. We find Jesus in a boat again, just as we left him in Matthew's Gospel. As a marvelous matter of fact, he is almost certainly in the same boat. You'll see Mark's parallel account of the parable of the sower earlier in the same chapter. Another clue is tucked in Mark 4:36. Catch how the evangelist says the disciples "left the crowd and took [Jesus] along since *he was in the boat*" (emphasis added).

The ESV makes it a little clearer: "Leaving the crowd, they took him with them in the boat, just as he was" (Mark 4:36). A hint that Jesus is about to take them a long, long way from home in a relatively short period of time is found in his own words in Mark 4:35. **What does Jesus say?**

Maybe the ominous feeling comes from knowing what is next, but the words seem to pick up the howling of the wind before we hear about the first gust. The reference to "the other side" will prove far more situational than directional.

Incidentally, what time of day was it?

The segment we're looking at today is a perfect script for a horror movie, all the way to the eeriness of starting in the dark. Even when a scary scene of a film or a book takes place indoors, have you ever noticed how no one thinks to hit the light switch? I like the adrenaline rush, the jumping out of my skin, and the bonding experience of the collective scream in a horror movie in a theater. I just don't want to actually live one. Today's lesson suggests that being in the same boat with Jesus doesn't mean we can't sail into something terrifying. It just means we're not sailing into anything without him.

The contrast between Jesus sleeping like a baby on a cushion in the stern and the disciples sopping wet and frantic on the bow is picture perfect. At no time does Jesus jump into our hysteria with us. At no time is he threatened by menacing conditions. And certainly at no time is he careless about whether we live or die. He's always with us in our storm, but never listless or restless.

The Sea of Galilee is a basin that drops well below sea level inside a wreath of hills and mountains, making it no stranger to storms. This squall, however, has more to do with disputed authority than topography. **How does Paul refer to Satan in Ephesians 2:2?**

The question the disciples ask Jesus may seem a bit dramatic, but it's quick to the tip of a panicking tongue.

Don't you care?

Jesus cared more than his disciples understood—and not only about them. He cared about a tormented soul with a storm howling inside him louder than the one tossing their sea. The fury Jesus invites you into may have little to do with you, beyond the opportunity for you to bear witness to the lengths Jesus will go to show his compassion. Now read Mark 5:1-13.

Place yourself in the scene alongside the disciples, climbing out of the boat with Jesus. Drawing from the information Mark records, describe what the man who suddenly appears looks like in your imagination.

Where had the man made his home?

Those of us who love meandering through an old graveyard reading headstones might agree that it's an acquired taste, shared primarily by history and ancestry lovers. Older individuals who have entrusted the bodies of many loved ones to such places also tend to find them considerably less spine tingling. This was no ordinary graveyard, however. No place for taking carnations or picking daisies. These tombs, for whatever reason, had become what any decent horror movie hopes to depict in a cemetery: a haunt of demons.

Not everyone who believes in Jesus believes demonic powers actually exist, but there's a solid reason to hold the traditional view: Jesus clearly believed it. This is the third time Mark gives ink to Jesus encountering and overruling demonic forces. Think metaphorically with me for a few moments. If Satan had his unhindered way, the living would incessantly cling to the lifeless. He would keep us in a perpetual loop of hope deferred, holding on to situations, positions, or relationships that are dead and gone. The cadaverous object could be a former job, a broken engagement, a passed-up opportunity, a pulseless friendship, a previous romance, a home foreclosure, a ministry partnership, or a faith community. Anything qualifies that has us collapsing our lungs trying to resuscitate a fossil.

We undoubtedly have a God of resurrection. But you and I need not cling to what is lifeless so we'll be close at hand should God decide to raise it. If God can resurrect the dead, he can also walk it to us. I never seem to get this lesson learned once and for all. Even recently God made this message resonant: *It's over, Beth. Let go.* **When was the last time you sensed something similar?**

If you happen to be there now, here's the coinciding truth: *You're* not over. The job may be. The relationship may be. The marriage may be. But you're not. You're still very much here. What God primarily wants to resurrect is you.

I interject these next few paragraphs lest I lead you to confuse a metaphor of living among the tombs with mourning the death of someone precious to you and/or visiting a grave. No situation in the human experience can strip the life from us like the death of someone we dearly love. Grief is not only appropriate in great loss, it is necessary for processing our sorrow, and no timetable can dictate how long it should take. Grief takes what it requires.

Satan doesn't want us processing our sorrow, however—and certainly not in company with the one who suffered and died and overcame the grave. The enemy wants us buried alive by it. If Satan can't get you to die *of* your grief, he'll do his best to see you die *in* your grief. **Does the difference make sense to you? If so, how would you explain it?**

Take a careful look at Mark 5:3-4. What facets of violence are implied?

Satan relishes seeing people out of control and cast out of community. Maybe, like me, you hurt not only for the tormented individual but also for those who potentially tried to help him. Maybe you feel for his family, like I do. When a midwife placed him in his mother's arms, she didn't look in his newborn face and see a legion of demons in his future. She saw hope. Beauty. Innocence. Love.

Mark 5:3 bleeds exhaustion from its pores:

No one was able to restrain him anymore.

Anymore. People had tried. And they'd failed. Maybe they'd been vicious and uncaring and tried to chain him up like a rabid dog. But maybe they'd done and done till they could do no more. Maybe he tried too. Resisted. Fought and lost. Not every defeat and every loss of family and community can be chalked up to the easiest answers in reach, like . . .

- It's his own fault. He didn't try hard enough.
- It's their fault. They just abandoned him.

Think how much the enemy of our souls must love the word *out*. Think how he'd exult in our being *out* of our right minds, cast *out* of our homes, put *out* of community, *out* of fellowship. He'd have us *out* of friends, *out* of options, *out* of words, *out* of provision, *out* of a place to go and a place to turn, entirely *out* of energy, *out* of answers, *out* of patience, wholly *out* of love, and summarily *out* of hope.

Who knows? Maybe the devil still has a chip on his shoulder, based on the implications of Revelation 12:7-9. **What does the disciple John see in this part of the revelation?**

In the furthest possible contrast, the New Testament letters speak of the redeemed as being "*in* Christ" nearly ninety times. An organization may throw us out. A school may throw us out. A circle of friends may throw us out. A place of employment may throw us out. A church may throw us out. A family may even throw us out. **But what does Jesus emphatically claim in John 10:28?**

Earlier in the same chapter of John, Jesus speaks of the thief who "comes only to steal and kill and destroy" (John 10:10). Mark 5 could hardly paint a more vivid picture of the thief when he has his way.

What heart-wrenching scene does Mark 5:5 sketch?

Satan delights in human self-hate and self-harm, and surely in large part because we're each image bearers of God and immeasurably loved by him. Let's not overreach the narrative and conclude that self-hate and self-harm are satanic and, worse yet, signal demon possession. Most of us have engaged in behaviors destructive to ourselves at times and likely even fostered the clear thought that, unabated and given enough time, they could be our complete undoing. We're within reasonable reach to simply conclude that Satan hopes they will be.

We'd have to go all the way back to the garden to grapple with the origins of why we humans are prone to do what could ultimately kill us. The world is broken by sin. Apart from God, the human condition is self-defeating. The mind is vastly complicated and, more often than we'd like to think, frighteningly fragile. The heart can also be crushed and woefully deceptive, telling us we are not worthy of seeking the help we need. We have brokenness we ourselves often don't understand. But God understands the origin of every fissure. He knows every avenue we need to take in order to heal. Satan doesn't care what a person's self-harm is rooted in. His main concern is taking advantage of it.

What was the name of the unclean spirit (verse 9)?

Why was it given this name?

Don't miss how the demonic principality has silenced its victim and taken up speaking for him. "Legion . . . because we are many." We have no way of knowing when the individual's nightmare began or how quickly his life was consumed by this army of demons. What the text conveys is how utterly overpowered he was. Scholar Robert A. Guelich writes,

> "Legion" appears as a Latin loan word in Greek and Aramaic texts which indicates how pervasive the concept was in the ancient world. A military term, it designates a unit or brigade in the Roman army including infantry and cavalry. The number varied between 4000 and 6000, but by Jesus' day and during the time of the empire the number appears fixed at approximately 6000 men of whom nearly 5800 were infantry.[6]

Recognizing the unrivaled power of Jesus, "Legion" knows exorcism is unavoidable. The only question is where the demons will be sent. **What request is made of Jesus (verse 12)?**

Fascinatingly, Jesus gives the unclean spirits permission to enter the herd of swine. How often—if ever—the disciples had seen such a herd is debatable since "Mishnaic law strictly forbade the Jews from raising pigs (m. B. Qam. 7:7)."[7] If I were in charge of the math here, I'd suggest the number of demons represented by "Legion" was about two thousand, to match the pig population, but if a legion could enter one man, I suppose one demon per pig is asking too little. Incidentally, no preacher in my entire upbringing could forgo a joke about deviled ham at this point in the message. It was standard. You just had to stomach it.

Their livelihood dashed into the sea, what did the herdsmen do next (verse 14)?

Write Mark 5:15 in this space.

He was transformed from the inside out by a man named Jesus from the far side of the sea. Luke's version says, "For a long time he had worn no clothes" (Luke 8:27). Maybe his garments were strewn in pieces among the tombs, but this doesn't seem very likely in view of the passage of time. So where did the clothes come from? Maybe Jesus had the disciples piece them together from extra clothing they had on, but on second thought, wouldn't they still be soaked from the storm? My imagination may be overactive, but I like to think Jesus gave the man his own outer robe, dressing him as God himself had dressed the man and woman in the garden in Genesis 3:21. And I believe the man, fresh in his right mind, could process the joy of it in resemblance to a prophecy he may have never even heard.

> I rejoice greatly in the LORD, I exult in my God;
> for he has clothed me with the garments of salvation
> and wrapped me in a robe of righteousness.
>
> ISAIAH 61:10

When the crowds gathered, the man the devil had possessed, harassed, and humiliated was found with sound mind, "sitting at Jesus's feet" (Luke 8:35). And it terrified them. Granted, pigs were big in the region of the Gerasenes. Jesus clearly wasn't good for their economy. But perhaps that's not all that frightened them. Do you know one thing that might have been scarier than the man losing his mind? Finding it.

What happened when Jesus was getting into the boat (Mark 5:18-20)?

If you're like me and we had our way, this story might end differently. I'd have the man throwing his leg over the side of the boat and climbing aboard right beside Jesus. I'd have thirteen disciples instead of twelve, all of them slapping him on the back, suiting him up, welcoming him to the team. But Jesus had more compassion than I do. He didn't just care about the man tormented by the legion of demons. He cared about the legion of people bereft of good news.

Jesus left the crowds, just as they begged him to. But not without leaving them a witness.

DAY 5

Some of those who were with us went to the tomb and found it just as the women had said, but they didn't see him.

LUKE 24:24

O Love that will not let me go
I rest my weary soul in thee
I give thee back the life I owe
That in thine ocean depths its flow
May richer, fuller be

GEORGE MATHESON

Open your Bible to the first chapter of Luke's Gospel and read verses 1-4. **Fill in all missing words, based on the CSB translation.**

It also seemed good to me, since I have ______________________________

____,

to write to you in an orderly sequence, most honorable Theophilus,

so that you may know the ____

of the things about which you have been instructed.

LUKE 1:3-4

Today we are going to follow Luke the beloved physician's lead and undertake an investigation. Think of it as a missing persons search. Most of the individuals in the snapshots of Scripture we've observed so far in our desire to know more about walking with God have been men. No issue there. We weren't trying to make a point regarding gender. Having entered the world of the Gospels this week, however, it would be irresponsible to ignore where Jesus himself appears to make a point regarding gender.

We're conducting a missing persons search today—not because women can't be found walking with Jesus, but because we haven't set out to find their footprints yet. Today's the day. We get to stand beside Jesus in various scenes where he's in the company of women, dignifying them in a world where they were largely dismissed, and in doing so, he no doubt got on a few people's nerves. I've found that Jesus doesn't mind getting on our nerves nearly as much as we might wish.

Jesus doesn't mind getting on our nerves nearly as much as we might wish.

All four Gospels record moments that don't just include women but illuminate them, to varying degrees, in Christ's radiant presence. To investigate all these moments would thankfully take days, so we will limit our search to Luke's Gospel and, even with this constraint, you'll have your hands full.

Before I send you to the primary places, bonus points if you are either ambitious enough or nerdy enough to take this challenge: Flip through the chapters of Luke and tally how many different women you find, whether named or unnamed. All you're looking for right now is a number. You won't be able to arrive at a precise sum because a few scenes reference women without specifying how many. **How many did you find?**

Rather than filing a missing persons report, think of the following document as a report of persons *found*. **Look up each of the following references to women or girls in the order they appear in Luke's Gospel. Fill in names where they're supplied, then check the context, recording the role (or place) of the woman or women in the scene. Where a name is not supplied but another identifier is used (i.e., widow), write it in the *Name/ID* blank. This exercise may seem daunting, but it will go faster than you think, and the result will be its own reward.**

LUKE 1:24, 36

Name/ID:

Role:

LUKE 1:27

Name/ID:

Role:

LUKE 7:13

Name/ID:

Role:

LUKE 7:37

Name/ID:

Role:

LUKE 8:1-3

Names/ID:

Roles:

LUKE 8:42, 54

Name/ID:

Role:

LUKE 8:43

Name/ID:

Role:

LUKE 10:38

Name/ID:

Role:

LUKE 10:39

Name/ID:

Role:

LUKE 13:11

Name/ID:

Role:

LUKE 15:9

Name/ID:

Role:

LUKE 18:3

Name/ID:

Role:

LUKE 21:2

Name/ID:

Role:

LUKE 23:49, 55

Names/ID:

Roles:

This final segment repeats several names mentioned earlier in Luke, but in view of its importance, go ahead and supply them and any other identifiers, then record the roles they filled.

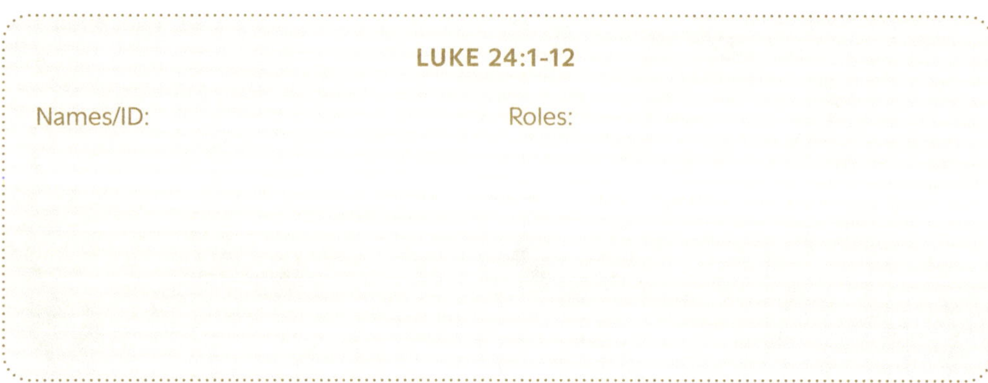

LUKE 24:1-12

Names/ID: Roles:

Reflect on what you've recorded from the Gospel of Luke. Don't rush. Behold the breadth, length, and depth of the montage of women who kept company with Christ.

In the Savior's conception by the Holy Spirit,
in the throbbing, quickening pangs of his birth,
in the traveling band, funding the journey,
in a patchwork of the sick cured and the dead raised to life,
in the quiet clang of a widow's coin,
in the scent of perfume from an alabaster jar,
on the floor at his feet, enraptured by his teaching,
in a fit of tasks and meal making, hosting half-perturbed,
in a bent body straightened on a Sabbath day, mid-sermon,
then,
in his suffering,
at his cross,
in his bleeding,
at his death,
in a tomb with no dead body,
and breaking news to the eleven who didn't believe a word they said,
women were there.
On purpose.

The Holy Spirit, who filled the pen of a beloved physician, made sure every attentive reader and hearer would know it.

These women were no mere bystanders. They were participants in the divine narrative. Envision them early that Sunday morning, with their minds spinning, their hearts broken, and their arms weighed down with spices for anointing Jesus' body, now a full weekend dead. We can't fathom their determination to care for him in his death as in his life without absorbing a fuller picture of what they came prepared to do. This wasn't only a cold, dead body they were going to view. This was a cold, dead body that had been pierced, beaten, and mangled beyond recognition—one they were about to tend to with their own bare hands.

To call these women fearless is to give them too little credit. Of course they were afraid. They proceeded anyway. Isn't this what courage is? Fidelity that exceeds our fears? Love incorruptible, braving whatever barbarity necessary? John's Gospel invites us into an almost unthinkable moment, the lens fastened on the face of one woman in particular.

> Standing by the cross of Jesus were his mother, his mother's sister, Mary the wife of Clopas, and Mary Magdalene.
>
> JOHN 19:25

His mother. No one would have blamed her if she sat this one out. Surely some who knew her tugged at her sleeve and tried to stop her from nearing the cross. "Don't put yourself through this." "It's too much." "Don't look!" But you and I both know a battalion of Roman soldiers couldn't have dragged Mary from that scene.

She'd taught Jesus to walk. And Jesus, in turn, taught her.

He'd taught her how to walk with God. This very God who came to earth in the likeness of humanity, the immortal made mortal, wounded flesh and spilled blood, hanging from a cross.

She'd swaddled the one they stripped. She heard the hammer hit the nails of the hands she'd held countless times in his toddlerhood to keep him out of harm's way. She'd taught the one the soldiers mocked how to say *Abba*. She was the first to whom he'd said the simple, ordinary words, "I'm thirsty." No, she would not be moved. She would not be shoved away. His mother would be there to the end. And maybe as she watched him suffer for unsparing hours, heaving himself up to draw every next breath, the end could not come soon enough. Lips moistened by sour wine, the son of Mary, Son of God, searched the air for one last gulp of oxygen and exhaled these words:

> It is finished.

The soldiers came to break his legs as they'd broken those of the criminals crucified beside him, but they found that Jesus was already dead. One of the soldiers took his spear and pierced the side of Jesus.

Nearly thirty-three years earlier, in the very city within Mary's peripheral view, a devout man by the name of Simeon had rejoiced at the sight of the infant Jesus cradled in her arms as she entered the Temple grounds for his dedication. Recognizing the child straightaway as the long-awaited Messiah, Simeon had taken him in his arms, blessed him, and praised God for letting him live to see the day he'd been promised. Imagine what glorious confirmation Simeon's words were to this couple who'd traveled arduous miles since Gabriel had first appeared to Mary. From this precipice of emotion, the young mother then heard Simeon make a statement that must have been startling—a statement she must have replayed in her mind countless times.

A sword will pierce your own soul.

LUKE 2:35

Delights

Perplexities

Sighings

Laments

Word Alerts

Divine Consolations/Comforts

Perceived Presence

WEEK 5

the SPIRIT *of* WALKING

SESSION 5

The Spirit of Walking

You can fill in these blanks as you watch the video for session 5.

Introduction: Our aim for the last four weeks has been to overview the biblical history of humans walking with God. We've drawn our attention to "The Beginning of Walking" in Genesis, "The Law of Walking" in the Books of Moses, "The Heart of Walking" in the Psalter, and "The Discipleship of Walking" in the Gospels. Today we break into the biblical era we live in—post-_____________ and pre-_____________—and gather our thoughts around the _____________ *of walking.*

1. Galatians 5:16-26 supplies us the most concentrated section of Scripture for our concept.

   . . . _______________________

   . . . ____________________________

   . . . ______________________________

   . . . _________________________ with the Spirit.

2. Where the journey with God begins for us: Ephesians 1:13-14.

   In him you also were sealed with the promised Holy Spirit when you _________________________________, the gospel of your salvation, and when _________________. The Holy Spirit is the down payment of our inheritance, until the redemption of the possession, to the praise of his glory.

3. A few considerations for tweaking our perspectives:

- Walking with God is not a _______________ to be _________________. It's an __________________ to be _____________________.
- Without margin, our walks with God will consist of _______________________ more than ____________________________.
- One way we learn to discern the leadership of the Spirit is ________________________.
- In this walk of faith, we keep our _______________ and pray our __________________.

4. A bold but biblically supportable claim: If we walk with God by the Spirit, we will ____________________, ____________________ live ________________________, including, at times, participating in the ________________________.

Sometimes we'll ________________________ it in ________________________.

Sometimes we'll ________________________ it in the ________________________.

Most times we'll ____________________ it in ________________________________.

________________________ we will ____________________ in ______________.

*Video session available for purchase at **TyndaleChristianResources.com**.*

Since this week is the final chapter in our study, your recordkeeping chart at the end of day 5 will serve as a reflection on your previous four charts. You'll find it on the page before the Epilogue. It will serve as your official conclusion. When you get to the recordkeeping chart, glance over the previous four charts, then based on those and/or your more meaningful moments during our five weeks, record your final takeaways as they correspond to each heading. Your "word alert" should be the verse from the study you associate most closely with it.

We leave the Gospels today, but let's promise each other we'll never let them leave us. We are incalculably blessed to hold in our hands the entire canon of Scripture, from Genesis to Revelation. It is the unfolding scroll of divine redemption. Every book is alive with the Holy Spirit, possessing keys to unlocking our understanding of God. Every genre in the Bible has a place in our equipping, in our fruit bearing, and in the renewing of our minds. Paul's words to Timothy will be just as true on the last day as they were the first day they were written.

> All Scripture is inspired by God and is profitable for teaching,
> for rebuking, for correcting, for training in righteousness.
>
> 2 TIMOTHY 3:16

Time cannot outlast God's Word. We're called to be students of all Scripture. But from the time we receive Christ as Lord until we stand in his presence, our lives are set apart specifically to bear witness to his life, death, and resurrection. We're told to adopt the same attitude toward humility, obedience, and sacrificial love that Jesus had. He bids us to deny ourselves, take up our cross daily, and follow him; to serve and not be served; to treat people as the image bearers they are; and to have active compassion on the marginalized. Throughout our lives of faith, God has one major objective: conforming us to the image of his Son.

We are the followers of Jesus. The most concentrated record of Christ's earthly ministry is found on the pages of Matthew, Mark, Luke, and John. We want to be immersed in the Gospels deeply enough that all else we read, study, process, and strive to understand is with our heads still dripping from our baptism into Christ.

Happily, Luke comes through with the perfect sequel for a smooth transition out of the Gospels into our final era. Welcome to "The Spirit of Walking."

DAY 1

God ascends among shouts of joy, the LORD,
with the sound of a ram's horn.

PSALM 47:5

. . . wonder, this excess of spirit brimming out of the body.

CHRISTIAN WIMAN

We'll take a comparatively short walk in Scripture today—just a little more than three-quarters of a mile—and, most notably, we'll seem to stop short of the best part. This stretch of ground has a vital place in our walk with God, however, because, without learning this lesson, we risk repeatedly missing the best parts.

Read Acts 1:1-14. The era we're discussing in our final week of this study takes its first toddle in Acts 1:12, with the disciples leaving the Mount of Olives and walking back to the city without the visible presence of Jesus. Go with them now to Jerusalem in your mind's eye. **According to the passage, how far do they walk?**

What a wonderfully Jewish detail from this Gentile physician's pen. The limit on how far a devout Jew could walk on the Sabbath was two thousand cubits, which is roughly three-quarters of a mile.[1] This distance was set in Numbers 35:5, according to the size of the pasturelands given to the Levites. Since Exodus 16:29 explicitly says people were not to exceed the perimeters of their land on the Sabbath, rabbis reckoned they were allowed to walk about the size of a pasture.[2] I find facts like these fascinating. This reference isn't indicating the ascension happened on a Sabbath. It's simply telling us how far they walked. If you invited me to go on a walk about the distance of a football field, for instance, I wouldn't think it was game night. I'd think we were going to take a six-or-so-minute stroll.

Renderings like "a Sabbath day's journey away" remind us that these Jesus-followers were devout Jews with no thought of starting some new religion. They were living the foretold continuance of Israel's story. They had not left their faith behind. They were carrying their faith forward to its glorious consummation in Christ. Let's walk down the Mount of Olives to the west, with a spectacular view of Herod's temple, but keep an eye on the path. It's a little steep in places. Make your way across the Kidron Valley, then take the large limestone steps up to a gate into the Holy City. Once you're within the wall, you'll know exactly where to go because you've been staying there at least since the crucifixion, and maybe since you arrived in Jerusalem for Passover. When you get to the place, you'll take the stairs to the second floor.

We have no way of knowing for certain, but this could be the same room where Jesus hosted the Passover with his disciples some forty days earlier. It might also be the home of John Mark's mother, since it was an established meeting place for early Christians—large enough for "many" people to congregate (Acts 12:12). This you can take to the bank: Whoever owned this home had considerable wealth.

Enter the room and look around, with Acts 1:13-14 in mind. Who do you find in the room besides the disciples?

What does Acts 1:14 record the group doing?

If those in the room were meeting quietly when the apostles returned, they were about to get quite the jolt. Imagine the ruckus. The disciples came back to the room and recounted what they'd just seen to others who weren't with them. **Maybe only a handful of people were**

present, but the total number could have been as many as _________, based on Acts 1:15. Luke 24:52 tells us the mood the apostles were in when they returned. Read it and record their frame of mind here.

Imagine that you and your friends in the faith just saw something so ridiculously wonderful, so utterly unimaginable, so consequential to the people you're informing that you all start talking at once, words tumbling out before your mind can even make sense of them. Maybe the scene went something close to this.

Someone in the room you've just entered says, "What do you mean, Jesus left in a cloud?"

You respond, "Just what we said! He was caught up in a cloud!"

They reach for something more recent: "Like on the Mount of Transfiguration, when three of his friends went up with him? And then the cloud evaporated, and there he was looking back to normal again, right? Did you see Moses and Elijah?"

You try to direct them to think even bigger: "No, we didn't see anybody with him! This was not like the Transfiguration—well, except for the cloud. We're saying his body lifted off the mountain—"

Your listeners naturally gravitate to gravity: "Come again?"

You'd get frustrated if your joy could be quenched. "Listen to what we're telling you! We all saw it! His feet literally came off the ground, and he just slowly kept going. And while he was speaking the blessing over us, a cloud wrapped around him and carried him right up into the air."

I like to imagine all the listeners jumping to their feet and running to the windows. As a friend of mine often says, you might as well be herding cats. You say, "He's already out of sight! But he's coming back."

They are, of course, right to ask, "Is that what he said?"

You clarify: "Well, yes, that's what he told us before his arrest, but this time it was two men in bright white clothing who suddenly showed up. They were the ones who told us."

Maybe this is when the women pipe up. "Oh, those two! We met them! Dazzling clothes? They were at the tomb. They were the ones who asked us why we were looking for the living among the dead."

Focus the lens once again on the familiar face in Acts 1:14. **After knowing where Mary stood at the end of week 4, what kinds of thoughts do you imagine are swirling through her head now, hearing of Christ's ascension?**

The Lord elected to leave us in the dark regarding what were surely three of the most meaningful, not to mention emotionally charged, post–resurrection encounters Jesus had. **Read 1 Corinthians 15:3-7. To whom did Jesus appear after God raised him from the dead?**

Who is this, according to John 1:42?

We have no way of knowing, of course, but in your thinking, why might Christ's first encounter with Peter after the resurrection have been best experienced privately?

Who else did Jesus make a point of encountering after his resurrection, according to 1 Corinthians 15:7?

This was the Lord's half-brother. These apparent one-on-one engagements could be viewed strictly as ministry appointments, since both Peter and James became pillars of the early church. But let's not hurry past James. Remember, none of Mary's sons believed in Jesus as Messiah and Lord until after the resurrection. James likely thought Jesus went to the cross as a tragically misguided figure with a Messiah complex, if not mentally ill. **Take a quick look at Mark 3:21. Why did Jesus' family try to restrain him?**

What, then, does seeing Jesus' brothers gathered in the upper room in Acts 1:14 say about the validity of the resurrection?

Maybe Jesus' encounters with both Peter and James were one-on-one primarily because they were none of anyone else's business. We want to know the goods. We want to hear what they said when they saw him. How embarrassed were they? Did they stumble over their words? Say how sorry they were? Whatever was said, Jesus kept that between them. I like to think he keeps some conversations between him and each of us private too.

While we know Jesus sought out Peter and James, we don't know if or when Mary got to talk to him by herself. What we do know is that she was in the upper room with the other women and her other sons. What we can imagine is that she took the news of his ascension and the assurances of his return uniquely. The sword that had pierced her soul could now become a sword in her hand—the certainty of divine promises kept, a tip to pierce the darkness, and a blade to slice through doubt. But wouldn't you imagine the wound it left in her soul was sore the rest of her life? Even if, God forbid, either of my daughters sustained a terrible trauma to their bodies and fully recovered, I can't imagine ever getting over the sight of their wounds.

Reflect on the gift God gave us in Jesus retaining his scars in his resurrected body. Scars are beautiful things, after all, aren't they? Heralds of healing, couldn't we say? They serve as signatures of the thorns of this fallen world, bearing testimony that we were fully here. None of us get through life without wounds. Sometimes our best hope is that all we have left are the scars, and it's a good hope. A sure hope that somewhere beyond our sight is a Healer.

In Acts 1:4, Jesus gave his followers very consequential instructions. What did he tell them to do?

As we near the conclusion of our journey together, we need a vivid reminder that waiting and walking are not mutually exclusive. They work in tandem. In fact, we can't learn to walk steadfastly with God if we never learn to wait, or we'll get ahead of the Spirit, fall on our faces, then demand to know why God didn't come through for us. The wonder in waiting on God is how often it is the antithesis of passivity. Waiting can be the hardest work we ever do, as evidenced in Katherine Wolf's story in this week's video.* Paradoxically, this work of waiting in hope is also how we regain fresh strength for the miles ahead (Isaiah 40:31).

We're still walking with God while we're waiting on God. We can make leaps and bounds of spiritual progress with the Lord while waiting for him to move in a way we know to follow. He's always coming, loved one. Always. The resurrection means that no matter how long the wait, he's always coming.

> We're still walking with God while we're waiting on God.

God will keep every promise he made. Use the wait to anticipate. Opportunity is ahead, and God wants us prayerful and mature enough to know what to do with it. Time is at Christ's full disposal. He'll use it to grow us, gird us up, give us vital life experience, and build us into people better fitted for the next juncture. Jesus told his disciples that the Holy Spirit comes with power. The Spirit is never impotent, incapacitated, or oblivious. If you belong to Christ, the Holy Spirit belongs to you, dwelling in you with a capacity beyond the fullest extent of your natural strength and skill. When we are yielded to divine authority, Jesus is made conspicuous in us, and we're counted among "many convincing proofs" that he is alive forevermore (Acts 1:3).

One last thought today. Don't you know Jesus' Father was glad he was on his way home? I hope Christ's reunion with the inhabitants of heaven is one of those moments we'll get to see replayed in his holy presence. Jesus was never out of his Father's sight, but he'd been a long way from the Father's side. The time had come. The thirty-three-year assignment was done.

*  *Find Beth's interview with Katherine Wolf here.*

That empty chair next to God's right hand was about to be filled. And I think the bounds of heaven throbbed and thundered and thrilled with anticipation.

In the magnificent prayer of Jesus recorded in John 17, just prior to his arrest, you can hear the yearning of Jesus, feverishly homesick for his Father.

> I have glorified you on the earth by completing the work you gave me to do. Now, Father, glorify me in your presence with that glory I had with you before the world existed. . . . I am no longer in the world, but they are in the world, and I am coming to you."
>
> JOHN 17:4-5, 11

Come home.

DAY 2

She doesn't consider the path of life; she doesn't know that her ways are unstable.

PROVERBS 5:6

The heart has its reasons of which reason knows nothing.

BLAISE PASCAL

Today's lesson invites us into Paul's magnificent letter to the Ephesians, where he makes more references to walking as a theological concept than in any other letter attributed to him. Before we look at several of those occasions, Ephesians 1:20-23 offers an irresistible bridge from day 1 and the emphasis on the ascension of Christ. **Using some of Paul's own wording, just how high did Christ ascend?**

You may not know what the miles before you hold or where Christ will have you go in the course of your earthly tenure, but you need never wonder where he is. Nothing can displace him. No one can replace him. **What does Ephesians 2:6 add to the picture?**

Jesus is seated in the heavens at the right hand of God while abiding with you here through the Holy Spirit. Likewise, you are seated with him there while abiding with him here through the Holy Spirit. These may be mysteries beyond human comprehension, but they make direct and very practical connections with how we walk on this terrestrial soil. The basic Greek verb the CSB translates six out of eight times as *walk* or *walked* in Ephesians is *peripateō* (περιπατέω), meaning literally "to walk about."[3] Scholar Francis Foulkes defines the word as "a 'walk,' a taking of step after step."[4] I like that, don't you? Depending on what translation you're using, you might find forms of the word *live* rather than *walk* in the verses we look up. Both interpretations serve the original term well.

Look up the four references labeled on this diagram and succinctly record below them what they say regarding walking.

Let's take a brief look at each of the four.

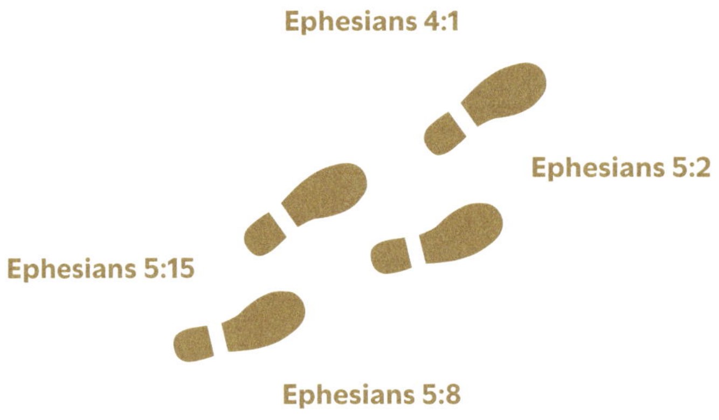

Walk worthy of the calling you have received.

EPHESIANS 4:1

To walk in a manner worthy of Christ's calling on your life is to walk in a way that reflects two overarching components: who you are and what you are. Sometimes when I'm swerving in my faith or having a crisis of identity, I'm served best by imagining God asking me directly, *Beth, who are you?* **Would you be willing to imagine the same question for a moment? If so, place your name in the blank.**

______________________, *who* are you?

Read Ephesians 5:1 and see who God says you are.

Now consider a second question, writing your name in this blank:

______________________________, *what* are you?

We could search the entire New Testament for an exhaustive list of ways to describe life in Christ, but Ephesians 1:3-7 contains a marvelous concentration that makes the point. **Comb through those five verses and write every word that depicts *what* you are. To get you started, your first word will be *blessed*.**

So what does it mean to walk in a manner worthy of Christ's call on our lives? Live like who you are—a dearly loved child of God—and what you are—blessed, chosen, holy, blameless, loved, predestined, adopted, graced, redeemed, forgiven. That is who and what you are. So "walk true to it," the Holy Spirit essentially says. If you need to write the truth of who and what you are with a permanent marker all the way up your arm until it finally sinks in, do it. This is your identity. The world's system and its prince, the devil, will do all they can to tell you differently. Counter every attack of identity with the truth.

Walk in love, as Christ also loved us.

EPHESIANS 5:2

Back up a few verses to check the context. **What does love look like in Ephesians 4:32?**

The attitudes and actions Christ has called us to seem impossible until we realize he's asking us to draw from the well of what we've been given. Think of it something like this:

You're dearly loved by God. Now love others out of that.

You're treated compassionately and tenderly by God. Now treat others compassionately and tenderly out of that.

You're deeply forgiven by God. Now forgive others out of that.

Can you imagine, then, how crucial it is that we believe and embrace how dearly loved and deeply forgiven we are? **How would a scarcity mentality affect our walk?**

At times, we function as if Jesus may have a big heart but he divides it up piecemeal to his followers, and some naturally get larger pieces than others. The truth is, Jesus gives his heart the same way he gave his life: fully and without reservation to each of his own. He says in John 15:9 that he loves his followers the way the Father loves him. All our trespasses were forgiven on the cross, not some. His heart is wholly compassionate toward us, not two-thirds compassionate and a third condemning. Embracing these truths is essential to expressing them to others.

Let's single out the word *forgiving* in Ephesians 4:32 for a moment. The Greek verb in this verse is *charizomenoi* (χαριζόμενοι), meaning "to give freely as a favor, give graciously."[5] Perhaps you're familiar with the Greek word *charis*, meaning grace. The term in Ephesians 4:32 is derived from charis, suggesting that forgiveness is a means of extending grace from the grace we've been given.

The road to spiritual maturity is marked in part by learning to trace our forgiveness of another person back to its source. Is it grounded in grace or guilt? Some of the most profoundly consequential cover-ups we'll ever hear about stem from guilt. Someone turns a blind eye to wrongdoing because they have also done wrong and they fear being uncovered or they're wrestling with unresolved guilt that has never led to true repentance. We cannot draw grace from our wellspring of guilt. Guilt can't bring grace. It can only excuse.

Remembering how God has graced us is vital to gracing others. Even under the Mosaic law, God told the Israelites through Moses, "You must not exploit a resident alien or oppress him, since you were resident aliens in the land of Egypt" (Exodus 22:21). **How, then, would you distinguish between letting people off the hook out of guilt and authentically forgiving people out of grace?**

Walk as children of light.

EPHESIANS 5:8

Widen the lens to Ephesians 5:3-14 for context. If we could grasp that God is not trying to cheat us but rather spare us, we'd save ourselves untold suffering. Humility spares us from the tremendous damage pride does to our character, careers, and relationships. Gentleness spares us from reaping the harshness we have sown. Forgiveness unlocks the prison door of bitterness and resentment. Perhaps you know from personal experience, as I do, the pain, chronic regret, and complications we can bring on ourselves through sexual immorality and the absence of healthy boundaries. God is gracious and merciful, and he used the excruciating consequences in my own life to bring me to a place of freedom, and I will thank him all the days of my life. But I want to say in no uncertain terms as this journey together nears its end, if you haven't been down that road, save yourself the inevitable anguish.

God is not trying to cheat us but rather spare us.

To be a person of light living in darkness is unfitting in the most literal sense: We don't fit there. We might think we do for a while, but the same pattern proves true again and again:

- The novelty wanes.
- Anxiety starts elbowing out the exhilaration.
- Covering becomes suffocating.
- Secrecy makes us sick.
- The Holy Spirit is increasingly quenched.
- Joy evaporates into the thin air of a windowless room.

If you could, what do you wish you could tell someone you fear is heading down a similar path?

The thing about that windowless room I mentioned is that it is not, in fact, doorless. As surely as Jesus walked out of the grave, you have a way out of that tomb. If, like me, you have been in a mess of your own making but you have not yet entrusted yourself to God's kindness and grace, believe this truth to your bones: You have not out-sinned God's lavish willingness to forgive you. You're simply not that powerful. Your sins cannot compete with the cross. What you've done wrong is a poor match for what he's done right. This doesn't mean our trespasses are no big deal. It means they aren't proportional.

You have not out-sinned God's lavish willingness to forgive you.

This gloriously unproportioned grace is what Paul is getting across to his reader in Romans 5:15. Look up the verse and fill in the blanks.

> The ________________ is not like the ____________________. For if by the one man's trespass the many died, ____________________ __________ have the grace of God and the gift which comes through the grace of the one man Jesus Christ overflowed to the many.

We'll conclude with the final exhortation you labeled on the diagram.

Pay careful attention, then, to how you walk . . .

EPHESIANS 5:15

"Not as unwise," Paul writes, "but as wise—making the most of the time" (verse 16). Only a few verses later in this same context, the apostle commends believers to sobriety rather than drunkenness and to the Holy Spirit as our thought-altering influence. Don't dismiss the mention of wine, but to make the best application to our present temptations, let's broaden our view. This twenty-first-century world offers a far wider menu of intoxicants than that of the first century. We have a host of options to numb, entertain, inebriate, and overstimulate us into mental oblivion. Addiction is epidemic.

Lest we form the wrong impression, sobriety in the Epistles isn't buttoned up and stern. It's an accurate and proportional view of reality, a gospel orientation earmarked by hope. Sober-mindedness communes freely with joy. It is well able to experience liberality. It just gets to miss the hangover. We're invited to enjoy the good things God has given and receive them with gratitude, but we're also told to keep our heads (1 Timothy 4:4; 2 Timothy 4:5). In the words of Paul's fellow apostle,

Be sober-minded, be alert. Your adversary the devil is prowling
around like a roaring lion, looking for anyone he can devour.

1 PETER 5:8

DAY 3

It's time for your interview with another person you respect about their walk with God. I've included sample questions here, but feel free to ask different questions, add to these, or change directions if something they say piques your interest.

Name:

Your relationship to the person:

Share a little about your childhood, particularly the dimensions that later impacted your walk with God, whether positively or negatively.

Were you involved in a church or any kind of community of faith in your upbringing? If so, tell me something about it.

How did you come to know Jesus?

Were you discipled in your early days of faith? If so, who were you discipled by and what did that process look like? If not, how did you find your own way with Jesus?

The reason I wanted to interview you is because, from my observation, your walk with God conveys authenticity and bears obvious fruit. Many people who come to know Jesus might not choose to walk with him in the kind of closeness you seem to. **What caused you to want to walk consistently and closely with God?**

What is the biggest difference walking with God has made to you?

Share a little about what walking with God looks like for you in the day in, day out routine. I'd love to have insight into how you practice some spiritual disciplines like prayer and Scripture reading. For example, how do you choose what segment you are going to read? Do you journal? I'd enjoy knowing about practices that nurture your walk with God.

What are a few resources besides your Bible that you find enriching?

Have you had the joy of close companions in your walk of faith? If so, have they been the same people throughout your life, or did different seasons bring different individuals?

If you could give only one piece of advice to someone beginning their journey of faith, what would it be?

Without feeling pressure to sound deep, name two of your very favorite things about Jesus.

DAY 4

Since we also have such a large cloud of witnesses surrounding us, let us lay aside every hindrance and the sin that so easily ensnares us. Let us run with endurance the race that lies before us, keeping our eyes on Jesus, the pioneer and perfecter of our faith.

HEBREWS 12:1-2

We are societal animals, by nature, when we experience a dissonance with what is around us, we feel diminished and threatened. It is as though we are estranged from all that previously enlivened us, and so our appetite for interaction wanes and loneliness sets in.

MICHAEL CASEY, *THE LONGEST PSALM*

As our road together nears its end, I close in on my own twelve-month preoccupation with this study. I've engaged in the other usual things throughout—family life, teaching events, travel, church, work, dogs—but this concept has held continuous sway in my thoughts. I can't say I'm happy to let it go, and I've also wondered what took me so long. In truth, I know the answer to that. To be remotely insightful when it comes to walking with God, miles aren't the only elements that need to accrue. So does the wear and tear of everyday living. So do the scars of failing and falling, tripping and tumbling. So do the blisters and bruises of human connecting. And, mercifully, so do the rhapsodies of renewal and recollecting.

When you get to be my age, you've experienced a good bit, and the firsts become fewer. But as I live and breathe, this has been one of the strangest years of my life. For the first time since toddlerhood, I experienced spells of being unable to walk. What I'm saying is, I couldn't feel my feet. Sometimes the numbness would spread to my legs. I began seeing doctors about back pain twenty years ago and learned my spine was degenerating prematurely. "You'll ultimately need surgery," they said.

"How will I know when?" I replied.

"When you can't stand it anymore."

That's the wrong thing to tell an individual with the determination of a bull moose. I was going to make it another day if I had to drag my body through it by my fingernails. Until this year. The degeneration became critical, the bottom vertebrae started collapsing on one another, and the compression narrowed the nerves practically to a pencil point. The pain grew excruciating. My legs and feet tingled constantly, like they were asleep, then all of a sudden, I'd have no feeling in them at all. I'd go for a walk in the woods and, without warning, lose sensation from my ankles down. I'd have to call Keith to get me while I held on to a tree. At events I had to have help getting up from my seat and to the podium to speak. This was not the body I knew.

I ended up on an operating table nine months into the year and can now boast all manner of hardware in my back. The surgeon says it's likely not the last surgery, but my gratitude knows no bounds for having my life back for now. To be sure, you may have experienced far worse. I bring up the subject for one reason: I've never in my life needed help walking until I began writing on walking. Call it coincidence if you like, but I think God wanted to make sure I didn't overlook a crucial point:

Sometimes we need the help of others to walk with God.

Sometimes, in fact, we're in such a state of emergency that we can't take another step without someone coming to our aid. Accompaniment is assumed in pilgrimage, where dangers abound and nights grow long. The New Testament letters testify relentlessly to the connectedness of believers. Paul calls some seventy-five different people by name. In 2 Corinthians 2:13 he tells of his distress over being unable to find Titus. In his final letter, he bids Timothy, "Make every effort to come before winter" and, surely with great affection for his dearest companion, says, "Only Luke is with me" (2 Timothy 4:21; 4:11).

We may have stretches of our journey when we're called to walk entirely alone with God, but those miles are mostly exceptional. The primary way of the walk of faith is pilgrimage. We are fashioned in the image of a triune God for fellowship. For community. And for close companions within that community. They increase our joys, soothe our fears, and comfort us in our sorrows. And they make us laugh. This is no small priority in my view. In an increasingly ailing world, no better prescription has ever been written than by Solomon:

A merry heart doeth good like a medicine.

PROVERBS 17:22, KJV

Indeed it does. We'll spend today on the theme of community, looking back to the Gospels first so the interactions of Jesus can be our prototype. **Read each of the following verses, and record in the blank the number of people listed or depicted, then if the information is given, write who they were:**

Luke 4:42: ____________________

Luke 10:1: ____________________

Luke 6:13: ____________________

Luke 9:28: ____________________

JESUS

Write each group of people from these Scripture passages in the rings, starting with the outside layer.

We'll contemplate each of these groups as representations in or around the community of faith.

The crowds: Think of this group as a mix of the curious, the seekers, and the followers. How common were crowds in the company of Jesus? You'd find forty-seven references to crowds of people in Matthew alone in the CSB, thirty-seven in Mark, forty-three in Luke, and nineteen in John. Did Jesus resent crowds? No. Did he take breaks from the crowds? Yes.

Jesus didn't need large gatherings to accomplish his work, but we'd be mistaken to assume crowds drew around him strictly for entertainment. I grew up during the era when megachurches were emerging as an indomitable force within American evangelicalism, advancing the idea that, if God was in it, it would be big. The thought was, *A big God does big things*. The pendulum of loudest opinion within my earshot has swung most recently the other direction: If the gospel is accurately preached and the Scriptures soundly taught, the numbers will be small. Crowds indicate compromise. **What is the take you most often hear in your sphere of interaction, and how do you think it developed?**

If our prototype is found in the New Testament, we're left to conclude that Jesus can do what he wants, anywhere he wants, with any number he wants. Picturing these groups as concentric circles, with Jesus as the center, let's move to the second largest number we find in the Gospels.

The Seventy-Two (or Seventy, depending on the translation): These were individuals equipped by Jesus to go into various communities, spread the message of his Kingdom, bring healing in his name, and serve as workers in fields of harvest. We'll let this group represent Jesus-followers in a somewhat organized community of faith. In the analogy we're drawing, this circle could correspond to a local congregation. Most congregations are marked by regularly scheduled gatherings of people who are pursuing a common goal (glorifying God through faith in Christ) and nurturing a common bond (spiritual growth and mutual encouragement in Christ) while being equipped to serve both within and without. **If you've had a positive experience of involvement with a local congregation, what made it most valuable? If you've had a negative experience, what was the worst part?**

The Twelve: Since this is the designation the New Testament gives to Christ's disciples, let's think loosely in terms of numbers but tightly in terms of function. Picture this group as people you go a little deeper with in knowing and obeying Christ and in the knowledge and application of Scripture than you would in a typical congregational gathering. The number varies, of course, and over time, so do the people, but the purpose of deeper discipleship remains the definitive characteristic in this inner circle. Some seasons afford more opportunity than others for meeting in smaller groups for deeper study, but the bonds that can form and the benefits that can abound are greatly worth the effort.

The Three: Within the inner circle of the twelve disciples, Jesus drew an innermost circle around Peter, James, and John, with himself at the center. These three were not set apart to be elites or to form a secret society or an exclusive brotherhood. They were summoned together by Christ to share companionship with one another and with him on the heights (the Transfiguration) and in the depths (the garden of Gethsemane) and in the miraculous (behind the closed door of a child's resurrection).[6]

Think of this group as a circle of your closest comrades in the faith—those you most deeply know and experience Christ with and those who have most deeply known you in Christ. In my own life, these are women I've gone to the heights and depths with, women who have walked with me through deaths and resurrections with Christ.

We might pick a discipleship group, but I think we'll find, especially in retrospect, that our closest companions in Christ seem picked for us by God. We wish we could cut to the chase, but the quickest way to make a person run for the hills is to take an approach like, "Hey, want to be my close companion?" The relationships represented by Peter, James, and John in this illustration are built, not manufactured. They take time and trust.

The best companions on our pilgrimage aren't our mirror images, because they develop more out of providence than preference. The people with whom we form our deepest bonds in Christ might not be of similar age or demographic. The common denominator need only be an earnest pursuit of Jesus as the ultimate priority. Sometimes relationships with the potential to be dearest to us are missed over preconceived notions of who and what they should be. **Do you have a fellow sojourner in your pilgrimage with Christ who came as a surprise to you? If so, in what way?**

Most of us yearn for these kinds of companions, but we can't shop for them like a used car. What we can do is ask God for them, seek out environments where Jesus-loving and -pursuing people can be found, serve genuinely among them, and invest the time that invites bonds to grow organically. How important is this innermost circle? When Jesus went into his agony alone with the Father, falling on his face, asking for the cup of death to pass from him, even he summoned his closest mates to a place nearby. We are fashioned for fellowship, even—and especially—in our sufferings. We need the kinds of companions who walk with us in the routine ups and downs and who are only a stone's throw away when we're alone in the depths with God.

In our walk with God, each of these circles of interaction has a place in the abundant life, even the crowds. When we lose touch with the curious and the seekers, we've closed ourselves in and lost our footing in Christ's commission. We thrive most when we interact within each of the four concentric circles. This is ideal, but the thing is, circumstances can make the ideal hard to come by. **Which one of the circles is currently most challenging or elusive to you, and why?**

A suggestion the older ones among us could offer from experience is to appreciate the gift of camaraderie, even if it's momentary. Seasons change. Circumstances change. People change. Closeness ebbs and flows. It comes in fits and starts. And sometimes it ends. We mortals are called to a lot of loving and a lot of letting go. The real work is to come to a place of gratitude for gifts we cannot keep.

But would you like to know something astonishing? We're already in remarkable company. Some of it we can see. So much of it we can't. We'll set aside the remainder of this lesson to imagine the company we already have but cannot yet see. **Read Hebrews 12:18-24.** The unknown writer of this compelling book draws a contrast between two situations involving nearness to God. Noting them will show us how we've come full circle since our second week's focus on "The Law of Walking." **What are the contrasting conditions?**

Fill in the missing words in Hebrews 12:22.

Instead, ______________________________

_________________ to Mount Zion . . .

Mount Zion looms above us in beauty and splendor, as surely as Mount Sinai rose like a giant in the wilderness after the exodus. Instead of warning, Mount Zion reverberates with "Welcome!" All boundaries are erased. All dread subsides. Instead of darkness, gloom, and storm, this peak shimmers with light and trembles with sounds of festal rejoicing, and shalom abounds like a sparkling river.

Using the illustration of the mountain below as a centerpiece, label every detail Hebrews 12:22-24 offers for what or whom is upon and around it. If you're feeling inspired, include illustrations.

Myriads of angels. Haven't we tried to imagine angels a thousand times? Haven't we marveled over fearsome heavenly messengers in places like the book of Daniel, where the seers dropped to the ground like they were boneless (Daniel 10:9)? Haven't we tried to picture the priest Zechariah's face in Luke 1, when Gabriel showed up out of the blue in the Holy Place? Then, some six months later, where might a young virgin named Mary have been when the same angel suddenly appeared to her? In her small home? Was he different at all in the two showings? Was he dressed the same?

In this Hebrews account, thousands and thousands of angels surround Mount Zion, the city of the living God, the heavenly Jerusalem we're drawing near to. I often recall what my missionary friend Carrie told me she heard while being airlifted to safety after her precious body sustained multiple gunshot wounds in Iraq. At the time, she didn't know she'd be the only survivor in the carload of missionaries that fell prey to terror.

From her hospital bed, she described to me the sound of what she instinctively knew was a chorus of angels singing. I asked what song, of course, and she said she didn't know, but it had the sound and feel of Black gospel music. This pleased me to no end. "But what was most marvelous, most otherworldly," she said, "was that I could hear each voice distinctively as they all sang together." Each voice was all its own yet in perfect harmony. I think of this almost every time I'm in corporate worship. I imagine God listening carefully for each of our voices. Each one is distinctive. Each one matters. He knows when one is missing. Forget what you sound like. Just sing your heart out. He's listening for you.

The assembly of the firstborn . . . the spirits of righteous people made perfect. There we are, and there we'll be. We'll finally find the perfect church, because we, with all our brothers and sisters redeemed by the blood of the Lamb, will *be* the perfect church, presented without spot or blemish or any such thing. And for the love of God, we'll all love each other.

DAY 5

A highway shall be there, and it shall be called the Way of Holiness;
the unclean shall not pass over it.
It shall belong to those who walk on the way; even
if they are fools, they shall not go astray.

ISAIAH 35:8, ESV

If I find in myself a desire which no experience in this
world can satisfy, the most probable explanation
is that I was made for another world.

C. S. LEWIS, *MERE CHRISTIANITY*

I wish I had the right words to convey what it means to me to have walked with you as we've sought together to walk more closely with God. The grace to serve you isn't lost on me. With all my heart, I thank you.

I thought about our journey a few days ago, reflecting on an amusing moment between my husband and me. I never go a day without walking in the woods near our home on the outskirts of Houston. I'm a nature junkie, and I watch for birds, stop for frogs, look for critters, and take endless pictures of deer. One of my favorite things to do on a walk is to count how many different animal tracks I can find. I came upon a large paw print I hadn't seen before, clicked a picture, and hightailed it home to show Keith. The man's a bigger nature nerd than I am, so he told me to take him to it posthaste. He got all the way down on his hands and knees, lowered his face about six inches from the ground, and gently blew the leaves away. He spent every bit of fifteen minutes on it, changing directions several times while trying not to disturb it. He pulled some change out of his jeans pocket to place in the pads of the print so he could study the proportions.

Finally he spoke up. "Yep, 'Lizabeth, this is a good find. Pretty sure it's a cat print. Maybe a bobcat, but if so, a big one. You may have fooled around and happened on a cougar print." I was so happy, I could hardly sleep that night.

I so hope you and I have come upon some good footprints in Scripture over these last five weeks. I hope we've taken the time here and there to get down on our hands and knees, our faces close to the ground, and study what we've found. This walk with you and the Lord has been meaningful to me. I pray it has been of value to you too.

We will spend our last lesson in Revelation 21 and 22, because there, toward the very end, we'll find the last set of footprints pressed by the Holy Spirit onto the sacred page. The name of the closing book of the Bible is taken from its opening verse: "The revelation of Jesus Christ . . ." (Revelation 1:1). "'Revelation' (*apokalypsis*) means to expose in full view what was formerly hidden, veiled, or secret."[7] It conveys an uncovering of some kind and could be used even in the context of lifting a lid off an object to view its contents.

Revelation was written as a circular letter entrusted by God to the apostle John during his exile on the island of Patmos and sent to seven first-century churches in a cluster of cities in Asia Minor. The book gives ink to some of the most moving scenes in all of Scripture and some of the most petrifying. Fascinating and fearsome, it begins and ends with the promise of blessing for those who read and heed it (1:3; 22:7).

Once upon a time, I would have offered you a concrete timeline for the events in the book and dogmatic interpretations of all imagery, symbolism, numbers, and visions, but you're about thirty years too late. Funny how we can get all the mysteries solved in our first Bible course, and the older we get, the more mysterious some things become. It's a relief, really. How burdensome to feel that all our interpretations have to be right. Part of growing is knowing we can be wrong.

Part of growing is knowing we can be wrong.

Now, don't misunderstand. I'm still game for great charts and rich discussions on marvelous moments in the book of Revelation and for tossing around a range of views in a lively class. For all that makes the book of Revelation daunting to navigate and fiercely difficult to interpret, one feature becomes beautifully clear once we know what we're looking for. It brings the beginning of the Bible full circle, to a perfect finish.

Before you embark on today's Bible reading, flip through the pages of your very first lesson in week 1. Note how we began with God creating the heavens and the earth. We launched "Walking with God" in the earliest chapters of Scripture, because the first reference to God strolling in the company of humans goes on record no later than Genesis 3:8. Beguiled by the serpent, the man and woman just ate fruit from the one forbidden tree.

The man and his wife heard the sound of the LORD God walking
in the garden at the time of the evening breeze, and they hid.

The man and woman God created had the privilege of walking with their Maker in the garden of Eden. This time, however, when God arrives on the scene to walk with them, they cover themselves out of shame and hide from God out of fear. If you took part in our opening video session, perhaps you'll recall this point: *Walking with God debuts as the antithesis of hiding from God.* The two actions—walking with God and hiding from God—are on opposing ends of the spectrum. **In succinct terms, what were the results of Adam and Eve's rebellion?**

Now, with Genesis 1–3 actively in mind, read Revelation 21:1-9 and 22:1-5, searching for every possible connection between the way the Bible begins and ends. Record them here:

Are any of these fresh considerations to you? If so, which ones?

You almost certainly caught the reference to the tree of life in Revelation 22:2. John makes an early reference to the tree of life that contains a significant word. **Read Revelation 2:7. Where is the tree?**

Scholar Alan F. Johnson makes the connection clearer: "'Paradise' (*paradeisos*) is a Persian loan word meaning 'a park' or 'a garden.' The LXX uses it to translate the Hebrew expression the 'garden' of Eden (Gen 2:8-10)."[8] (The LXX is a reference to the Septuagint, an ancient Greek translation of the Hebrew Old Testament.)

A new heaven and a new earth. God dwelling with humanity. The previous things have passed away. Death has died. All grief, crying, and pain have subsided. The eternal Lamb of God—the "last Adam" of 1 Corinthians 15:45—comes down with his bride. And there it is: the tree of life that was locked away from humanity since that fateful day. There are leaves once again—not for covering but for healing, and not for a couple but for the nations. There is no longer any curse. No longer any night. No need for lamp or light, "because the Lord God will give them light, and they will reign forever and ever" (Revelation 22:5).

A Jewish hearer in John's day would catch allusions to the Hebrew Scriptures again and again in Revelation. The Ark of the Covenant and the plagues, for example, call Exodus to mind. Much of the imagery in Revelation hearkens back to books bearing the names of Old Testament prophets like Daniel and Zechariah. Some of the most magnificent passages in Revelation depict worship in a psalm-like cadence.

But how about that final appearance of the word *walk* I promised you? You'll find it tucked within the description of the new Jerusalem. **Read Revelation 21:22-27. What will illuminate the city?**

What will "walk by its light"?

And who "will bring their glory into it"?

As you read the next several paragraphs, circle any appearance of the word *nation(s)*.

After the fall of humanity in the garden in Genesis 3 and the flood in Genesis 7, the earth was replenished, nations emerged, and a migration occurred. Humans united, but for no mere unity, nor for peace, equity, or benevolence. They sought strength in numbers only for the purpose of building "a city and a tower with its top in the sky" to reject their Maker's way and make a name for themselves (Genesis 11:4). The Lord scattered them across the earth, then called a man named Abram from an idolatrous people. He announced to him, astonishingly, that all the nations would be blessed through him (Genesis 12:3). This declaration was the unbreakable cord of a covenant of promise woven throughout the fabric of God's eternal plan. Thousands of years later, an apostle named Paul, inspired by the Holy Spirit, claimed this blessing extended to the nations through Abraham's seed to be the gospel preached "ahead of time to Abraham" (Galatians 3:8).

This divine promise would find its fulfillment through Jesus, the Son of God and heir of salvation:

> Existing in the form of God,
> [he] did not consider equality with God
> as something to be exploited.
> Instead he emptied himself
> by assuming the form of a servant,
> taking on the likeness of humanity.
> And when he had come as a man,
> he humbled himself by becoming obedient to the point of death—
> even to death on a cross.
> For this reason God highly exalted him
> and gave him the name
> that is above every name,
> so that at the name of Jesus
> every knee will bow—
> in heaven and on earth
> and under the earth—
> and every tongue will confess
> that Jesus Christ is Lord,
> to the glory of God the Father.
> PHILIPPIANS 2:6-11

In Revelation 7:9, John sees a vision of "a vast multitude from every nation, tribe, people, and language, which no one could number, standing before the throne and before the Lamb." Revelation comes to a conclusion in the final chapters of Scripture, then, with the image of the redeemed from the nations walking by the light of God's glory and the lamp of the Lamb, with every earthly authority bringing honor and glory to the One and Only who is worthy.

All rebellion has met its end. All idolatry, corruption, depravity, and deception have ceased. The tyrants, the powermongers, and the greed-driven who have oppressed, starved, enslaved, imprisoned, exploited, and killed the people of God (whom God tallies one by one) will be judged and cast out forever. The bloodthirsty, the vile and violent, the abusers and false accusers will be no more. The vulnerable will no longer fear the darkness, for there will be no more night. All wicked rule and all that is cruel will fall away into some distant past that no longer holds any power over us. The prayer of the ages taught to the church by their King will finally be answered.

Christ's Kingdom will have come, his will having been done, on earth as it is in heaven.

Every promise kept. Every prerequisite met.

Behold! "God's dwelling is with humanity, and he will live with them. They will be his peoples, and God himself will be with them and will be their God. He will wipe away every tear from their eyes" (Revelation 21:3-4). Scripture isn't saying every tear will suddenly dry. The rivers of sadness, pain, and grief that have streamed down the faces of mortals through the ages will not merely evaporate. They will be wiped away by the hand of God. I have to believe this to be the tender, nail-scarred hand of Jesus. If you've pondered the multitudes depicted in the new heaven and the new earth, and wondered if you will ever come face-to-face with Jesus—just the two of you—rest assured: You will see his face, and he will see yours. And in that moment, he will see every tear you have ever cried and he will lift his gentle hand and wipe them all away.

And we, the ransomed and redeemed of all generations, will walk with Jesus in his glorious garden. We can walk barefoot, if we want, for the soles of our feet need not fear thistle or thorn. They will press into the soft, rich soil of a new earth, and everlasting joy will be upon our heads.

Delights

Perplexities

Sighings

Laments

Word Alerts

Divine Consolations/Comforts

Perceived Presence

Epilogue

Months have passed since I wrote the last sentence of this study and recorded the wrap-up video. As I was writing, the multiple incisions on my back and side were finally getting less tender to the touch. I was healing up from spine surgery and finding my footing again, head still spinning from the uncanny timing. Nothing was more forthright on my mind than walking, both spiritually and, as it turned out, *physically*. To call it coincidence seems an insult to providence.

We live our Christian lives believing the biblical truth that Christ is always with us, yet have you also noticed how, every now and then, he proves so unmistakably intentional about making his presence known, it's rattling?

Eight months after spine surgery, I went back under the knife to have both knees replaced. I knew it was coming. The neurologist told me I very likely had other surgeries coming. The spine, hips, and knees are inextricably linked, requiring a certain amount of alignment to function correctly. Let one get out of kilter and leave it unaddressed, and the others will eventually follow.

So the second round of major surgery was a good thing. In fact, I was told that coupled with the previous procedure, if I attended faithfully and carefully to yet another several months of physical therapy, I stood to regain agility I hadn't had in years. The prospects were great. The process was brutal. Those first five weeks, the pain was unrelievable. I never regretted the surgery. I never even wished I'd had the knees done at different intervals. I wanted to get it over with. I was willing to do the work—I simply hadn't anticipated *how much* work. You see, the problem with knee problems is how much you need knees to actually walk. There I was again, wincing and reeling, trying to put one foot in front of the other.

I began writing *Walking with God* eighteen months ago, my convictions strong, my heart full of anticipation, knowing that nothing in my entire life had been as satisfying, lifesaving, sanctifying, and joy-giving as journeying with Christ. Of course, there have been steep climbs and deep tumbles, but this walk has been life to me. The name of Jesus was as familiar to me in childhood as the names of my brothers and sisters. The way I saw it, for the most part this study was already written in the reaches and recesses of my mind. It would materialize primarily from the gentler graces of past experience. All I had to do was pray it onto paper.

I think maybe the way the Lord sees it, the past is only as useful as it is rinsed of nostalgia. You can't teach about walking with God from sentimentality. It's too flimsy. Too misleading. You need fresh reminders of how sharp the rocks on the path can be, how blind the turns, how dark the nights, how quiet the voice, and how crucial the faith.

Facing the second surgery, the question looming in the clouds seemed to be this: *How much pain are you willing to endure to be significantly healed?*

I'd dealt with chronic pain to varying degrees since my mid-forties. The thought of it getting remarkably worse before it got better was as thrilling to me as being stampeded by a herd of laughing hyenas. So my retort to the heavens was this: *Could we just count time served?*

Clearly the answer was no. If the physical therapy after my spine surgery was hard, the rehab for my knees was torturous. The prescription in three words? *Move, move, move.* If you sit still, you freeze up, and nothing, my friend, hurts worse after knee surgery than getting up after freezing up.

I tried to look on every possible beam of the bright side. "Will I regain my previous height?" I'd been unable to straighten my legs completely for several years, shortening the tape measure from five foot five inches to a little over five foot three inches.

"It's possible!" the nurses said. I determined that, if it were possible, then, by doggies, it was probable. I'd like to go on record saying nobody told me how bad it would hurt to take back those two inches. The new joints came with the capability to press the back of my knees flat to the floor—legs straight as arrows—but the old muscles had to relearn a skill they'd long forgotten. The physical therapists would strap my leg into an apparatus that would hold it straight and set the timer for a few mere minutes. It took all the self-control I could muster not to scream at the top of my lungs.

I'd stand at the bottom of a set of stairs at the sports medicine center early in my rehabilitation, and the therapist would say, "We're soon going to climb those stairs." It may as well have been Mount Everest. The day finally came. She wrapped a belt around my waist, steadied me from the back, and up we went. Then down. Then up again. And down again. "Don't be scared. I've got you." And she did. We walked the indoor track a hundred times—forward, backward, sideward. We did knee bends, ankle bands, leg lifts. They put me on the bicycle, and then a few weeks later, graduated me to the elliptical. We worked and worked and worked.

Here's the wild part. Remember when I told you in the introduction to our series that I walked with a limp? I wasn't ashamed of it. It was what it was. I'd had it for years. It was part of me. Well, the thing is, I don't have that limp anymore. I wouldn't have thought it was possible at my age. I used to have to hold on tight to a rail to walk up and down the stairs. I don't have to do that anymore either. I don't know what to make of it. If someone doesn't stop me, I may have a mind to circle back to the church gym and teach aerobics again.

I'd limit all this to my prayer journal if I didn't think God might have something in it for you. I wonder if you, too, have assumed that certain afflictions, infirmities, or limitations are a permanent part of you and you'll carry them to your grave. We both know healing on this side of the veil is only temporary. These bodies of ours will wear out. But what if, in scooting closer to walk with God, learning from leaning, you received some kind of blessed reprieve? A decades-long hindrance removed? Or a deeply set fissure healed? What if, in asking for your complete reliance, Jesus brought you a whole new confidence?

Five weeks after both knees were replaced, I finally got to drive to the grocery store by myself. The freedom felt fabulous, but no sooner had I rolled a grocery cart twenty feet down the dairy aisle than I caught myself forgetting the posture I'd worked to regain and hunching over the cart. A voice inside me chided, *You don't have to do that anymore, Beth! You don't need to hold on. You don't need to limp! This is no longer a condition to endure. It's now a habit to break.*

Maybe it was me reminding myself. Or maybe it was the Holy Spirit. Either way, I credit the Lord, because it was the gospel truth. The healing had come, but the habits were still there, especially when I was tired and no one was looking. I wonder if you can relate.

That's the way it is sometimes on the journey of faith, don't you think? He's with us in all that crushes us, all that stoops our shoulders and breaks our legs. And there's no shame. No condemnation. No harsh judgment. We're tenderly loved in our frailty. Divinely strengthened in our weakness. Graced in our need. We're not an atom more loved when we're soaring like eagles. And God may see fit that we walk with him in affliction or infirmity all the way home. Leaning and learning. Learning and leaning. He does not love us less because he healed us less. We'll all be whole at the first glimpse of him anyway. But now and again, God may set aside an unexpected stretch of miles for some hearty rehabilitation and require us to give him everything we've got.

Move, move, move.

Up the stairs and down again. Don't be scared. I've got you.

Walk with me. Closer now, closer. Endure the pain.

You're going to like how this turns out.

SESSION 6

Wrap-Up

You can fill in these blanks as you watch the wrap-up video.

Having spent all this time together turning the pages of Scripture and talking about walking with God, and having introduced you through interviews to some individuals whose journeys I've admired, I thought perhaps I'd take a different approach in our farewell and talk to you directly, with no stage or crowd or special guests.

Three final reminders before we go our separate directions with God:

1. ________________ like it's the ______________ ________________ of living.
   Because ______________ ______________.

   See Philippians 1:9.

   Consider Psalm 25:15.
2. ________________ like you know ____________ ____________ __________.
   Because ______________ ________________.

3. Hold __________ ____________ _________ like __________ ______________.
   Because ______________ ________________.

Godspeed, beloved of Christ Jesus. What a privilege to serve you.

*Video session available for purchase at **TyndaleChristianResources.com**.*

Notes

INTRODUCTION: THE WALK AHEAD

1. Brother Lawrence, *The Practice of the Presence of God: Being Conversations and Letters of Nicholas Herman of Lorraine* (Martino Fine Books, 2016).
2. Eugene H. Peterson, *First and Second Samuel* (Westminster John Knox Press, 1999), 6–7.

WEEK 1: THE BEGINNING OF WALKING

1. James A. Swanson, *A Dictionary of Biblical Languages with Semantic Domains: Hebrew (Old Testament)* (Logos Research Systems, 1997).
2. John Foxe and The Voice of the Martyrs, *Foxe: Voices of the Martyrs: AD 33–Today* (Salem Books, 2001), 120.
3. Foxe and The Voice of the Martyrs, *Foxe: Voices of the Martyrs*, 120.
4. Robert Alter, *The Hebrew Bible: A Translation with Commentary* (W. W. Norton, 2018), 11.
5. C. H. Spurgeon, Sermon No. 2147, June 1, 1890, Metropolitan Tabernacle, Newington.
6. Gordon J. Wenham, *Genesis 1–15*, Word Biblical Commentary, vol. 1 (Word, 1987), 169.
7. Wenham, *Genesis 1–15*, 169–170.

WEEK 2: THE LAW OF WALKING

1. John I. Durham, *Exodus*, Word Biblical Commentary, vol. 3 (Word, 1987), 136.
2. Durham, *Exodus*, 86.
3. Durham, *Exodus*, 39.
4. Douglas K. Stuart, *Exodus*, The New American Commentary, vol. 2 (B&H, 2006), 346.
5. Timothy R. Ashley, *The Book of Numbers* (Eerdmans, 1993), 185.
6. W. A. Vangemeren, "Shekinah," in Geoffrey W. Bromiley, ed., *The International Standard Bible Encyclopedia*, vol. 4 (Eerdmans, 1995), 466.
7. Paul J. Achtemeier, *Harper's Bible Dictionary* (Harper & Row and Society of Biblical Literature, 1985), 938.
8. H. G. Stigers, "Dwell," in C. F. Pfeiffer, H. F. Vos, and J. Rea, eds., *The Wycliffe Bible Encyclopedia* (Moody Press, 1975).
9. George R. Beasley-Murray, *John*, Word Biblical Commentary, vol. 36 (Word, 1999), 14.
10. Jeffrey H. Tigay, *The JPS Torah Commentary: Deuteronomy* (Jewish Publication Society, 2003), 76.
11. David H. Stern, *Complete Jewish Bible* (Messianic Jewish Publishers).
12. Ellen F. Davis, *Opening Israel's Scriptures* (Oxford University Press, 2019), 107.

WEEK 3: THE HEART OF WALKING

1. Ellen F. Davis, *Opening Israel's Scriptures* (Oxford University Press, 2019), 312.
2. Marvin E. Tate, *Psalms 51–100*, Word Biblical Commentary, vol. 20 (Word, 1998), 21.
3. J. R. R. Tolkien, *The Hobbit* (75th Anniversary Edition, Kindle).
4. Tolkien, *The Hobbit*.
5. Tolkien, *The Hobbit*.
6. Malcolm Guite, *The Word Within the Words* (Fortress Press, 2022), 37.
7. Gerald H. Wilson, *The NIV Application Commentary: Psalms—Volume 1* (Zondervan, 2002), 341.
8. Derek Kidner, *Psalms 1–72: An Introduction and Commentary*, Tyndale Old Testament Commentaries, vol. 15 (InterVarsity Press, 1973), 108–109.
9. Spiros Zodhiates, ed., *The Complete Word Study Dictionary: New Testament* (AMG, 2000).
10. Katie M. Heffelfinger, "Truth and Hidden Things: Reading Isaiah 45:9-25 as Scripture," in Stephen D. Campbell et al., eds., *A New Song: Biblical Hebrew Poetry as Jewish and Christian Scripture* (Lexham Academic, 2023), 156.

WEEK 4: THE DISCIPLESHIP OF WALKING

1. Thomas R. Schreiner, *1, 2 Peter, Jude*, The New American Commentary, vol. 37 (B&H, 2003), 251.
2. W. W. Wessel, *Mark*, in F. E. Gaebelein, ed., *The Expositor's Bible Commentary: Matthew, Mark, Luke*, vol. 8 (Zondervan, 2010), 622.
3. James R. Edwards, *The Gospel According to Mark* (Eerdmans, 2002), 23.
4. N. Clayton Croy, "Commentary on Mark 14:1–15:47," Working Preacher, April 5, 2009, https://www.workingpreacher.org/commentaries/revised-common-lectionary/sunday-of-the-passion-palm-sunday-2/commentary-on-mark-141-72-151-47-2#:~:text=It%20has%20often%20been%20noted,the%20story%20of%20Jesus'%20passion.
5. Spiros Zodhiates, *The Complete Word Study Dictionary: New Testament* (AMG, 2000), 1343–1344.
6. Robert A. Guelich, *Mark 1–8:26*, Word Biblical Commentary, vol. 34A (Word, 1989), 281.
7. Guelich, *Mark 1–8:26*, 281.

WEEK 5: THE SPIRIT OF WALKING

1. John B. Polhill, *Acts*, The New American Commentary, vol. 26 (Broadman & Holman, 1992), 88.
2. F. F. Bruce, *The Book of the Acts* (Eerdmans, 1988), 39–40.
3. A. S. Wood, "Ephesians," in F. E. Gaebelein, ed., *The Expositor's Bible Commentary: Ephesians Through Philemon*, vol. 11 (Zondervan, 1978), 34.
4. Francis Foulkes, *Ephesians: An Introduction and Commentary*, Tyndale New Testament Commentaries, vol. 10 (InterVarsity Press, 1989), 77.
5. Frederick William Danker, ed., *A Greek-English Lexicon of the New Testament and Other Early Christian Literature*, 3rd ed. (University of Chicago Press, 2000), 1078.
6. See Matthew 17:1; Matthew 26:37; Mark 5:37.
7. Alan F. Johnson, "Revelation," in Frank E. Gaebelein, *The Expositor's Bible Commentary: Hebrews Through Revelation*, vol. 12 (Zondervan, 1981), 416.
8. Johnson, "Revelation," in *The Expositor's Bible Commentary*, 436.

About the Author

Author and speaker **Beth Moore** is a dynamic teacher whose conferences take her across the globe. Beth founded Living Proof Ministries in 1994 with the purpose of encouraging women to know and love Jesus through the study of Scripture. She has written numerous bestselling books and Bible studies, including *So Long, Insecurity*, *Chasing Vines*, *Breaking Free*, *Entrusted*, *Now That Faith Has Come*, and *The Surpassing Value of Knowing Christ*, which have been read by women of all ages, races, and denominations. Readers were charmed by her first work of fiction, *The Undoing of Saint Silvanus*, and her memoir, *All My Knotted-Up Life*, received the Christian Book of the Year Award from the Evangelical Christian Publishers Association. Many of her teachings can be found on her YouTube channel, *Living Proof Ministries with Beth Moore*.

Beth and her husband of forty-seven years reside on the outskirts of Houston, Texas. She says of their two adult daughters, "To imperfectly raise little girls into women who become your best friends is a drenching fountain of God's grace." Beth and Keith have an armful of grandchildren and their hands full with Pecos, their precocious bird dog.

CONTINUE YOUR WALK WITH GOD
THROUGH THE BEAUTY AND WONDER OF NATURE

Accompanied by awe-inspiring full-color photography from landscape cinematographer and visual artist Stephen Proctor, whose photography is featured throughout *Walking with God*, the book *Wild Wonder: What Nature Teaches Us About Slowing Down and Living Well* combines pastoral observations about creation with an exploration of how it can provide healing to our minds and bodies.

Learn more at wildwonderbook.com.

CP2089